A Tale of Two Confessions

The 1ˢᵗ & 2ⁿᵈ London Baptist Confessions

Stuart L. Brogden

2025

Historical and theological development of these two confessions, with a comparison of content and analysis thereof.

A Tale of Two Confessions

The 1ˢᵗ & 2ⁿᵈ London Baptist Confessions

by Stuart L. Brogden

Printed in the United States of America

ISBN: 978-0-9986559-8-7

PUBLISHED BY:

Brogden's Books

https://brogdenbooks.blogspot.com/
brogdensbooks@gmail.com
La Vernia, TX 78121

All Scripture references are from the Holman Christian Standard Bible (HCSB) unless otherwise noted.

Table of Contents

Endorsements

Many claim there is no distinction between the First and Second London Baptist Confessions, much as covenant theology teaches continuity between the Old and New Covenants. However, Stuart presents a compelling counterargument, revealing the stark contrasts that exist between the two confessions, particularly regarding the Law of Moses. With clarity and insight, Stuart takes readers on a fascinating journey, exploring the distinct sources each confession drew upon, and the vastly different historical contexts that developed in the forty years separating their creation.

But that's not all—Stuart's exploration doesn't stop at the surface. The appendices alone offer a treasure trove of thought-provoking material: the Anabaptist influence on the early Baptists, the so-called "Christian" Sabbath, the Law of Christ, and the intriguing debate over holy people versus holy days. These sections are rich with insights that make the book a must-read.

In penning this enlightening comparison, Brother Brogden has truly served the Bride of Christ, offering a refreshing and much-needed perspective that challenges assumptions while deepening our understanding of the differences between the true covenant of works (the Mosaic Covenant) and the actual covenant of grace (the New Covenant).

Stephen Atkerson
President, NTRF.org (Early Church Practice, Today!), Baptist Elder, and Author, *New Testament Church Dynamics*

A Tale of Two Confessions is a compelling historical and theological examination of the 1644 and 1689 London

Endorsements

Baptist Confessions, written with clarity, depth, and a commitment to biblical fidelity. Stuart Brogden provides a balanced yet critical assessment of how these confessions developed in response to their historical and theological contexts.

Unlike many academic treatments that assume the 1689 Confession as the Baptist standard, Brogden challenges this assumption and provides a historically conscious argument for why the 1644 Confession should not be dismissed. He rightly reminds us that confessions serve as aids to understanding rather than authoritative grids through which Scripture must be read. His commitment to keeping Scripture as supreme over any human tradition aligns well with New Covenant Theology's emphasis on Christ as the final and ultimate revelation of God's will.

A Tale of Two Confessions is a must-read. It challenges readers to think biblically rather than merely traditionally, making it a valuable resource for pastors, theologians, and serious students of Scripture.

Louis Lions
Pastor, New Covenant Church
Sugarland, Texas

I am not a lover of history. But Stuart has succeeded in not only capturing and holding my attention, but also in providing an understanding of the crucial differences between the various Baptist confessions of the 17th century. He manages to provide a wealth of enlightening information, not only as to content, but as the raison d'etre for the variations. This useful volume exposes clearly that creeds and confessions are products of their times – they have a historical context which determines what is written in them.

Secondly, Stuart states boldly that such documents are the products, however sincere and honourable, of men's minds, and as such must be subjected to God's authoritative word and not the other way around. Stuart writes in a non-compromising fashion, yet with great sympathy towards those who were compiling statements about their faith which were often attempts to plead for life and freedom as well as belief.

I heartily recommend *A Tale of Two Confessions* - to academics and non-historians such as me alike.

David White
Currently serves as an Elder in his church on the South coast of the UK. He also seeks to provide an active online presence to uphold Biblical truth in the Facebook group New Covenant Grace and his own blog, White-erings.blogspot.com

Do we really need another book of Baptist Confessions of Faith? Yes, particularly if it's a book which is thoroughly researched, well written and aims to give the reader a clearer understanding of Baptist confessions, comparisons, history and theology behind them.

While some Christians reject the use of confessional statements (in part or in whole), Stuart clearly explains that 'all' Christians are a 'Confessing People'. In fact, his opening statement clearly shows why some do not support the use of confessional statements; "*The Confessions published by the Baptists in the Seventeenth Century were neither creeds written to secure uniformity of belief, nor articles to which subscription was demanded.*" It is the potential abuse of confessional statements which deter some from using them.

Endorsements

Citing the great 19th century preacher, Charles Haddon Spurgeon, these confessional statements are "*not issued as an authoritative rule, or code of faith, whereby you are to be fettered, but as an assistance to you in controversy, a confirmation in faith, and a means of edification in righteousness.*"

Beginning with the background for the 1644 LBC helps one better understand the reason for and the correct use of this confessional statement. Christians are often misquoted and/or misrepresented in their true beliefs. Stuart walks us through the historical and theological background explaining the purpose for creating the confession.

"*A Tale of Two Confessions*", while focused primarily on the 1644 & 1689 confessions, illustrates the comparisons and differences between these two documents and others. Baptists of the 17th century, in particular, experienced much persecution for what they did and did not believe. Confessional statements were far more than a commentary of what they believed, but a testimony to true Biblical teaching. Stuart's impeccable research and concern for the 'proper' place for confessional statements is a must read for every Baptist who are people of the Bible.

Sam Hughey
https://www.reformedreader.org/

Stuart has filled a void by writing this book. Like I mentioned to him several years ago, if the 1644 London Baptist Confession were better known I would use it more than the 1689. Wherever one stands on this, it is our duty as students of the Word of Truth to study all of our Baptist Confessions in light of the Bible. Read and learn. Thanks, Brother Stuart, for another great work!

A Tale of Two Confessions

Tom Lassiter
Pastor of Crestview Baptist Church
Big Spring, Texas

A Tale of Two Confessions; Stuart Brogden gives us a refreshing addition to the Baptist-history library, challenging the Reformed Baptist/Covenant Theology historiography. History, as Brogden implies, is messy. The Reformed Baptist model, on the other hand, reads Baptistic history as rather monochromatic and predictable. He provides a comprehensive, well-researched, argument that the 1644 London Baptist Confession of Faith was not inevitably an early form of Covenant Theology. Many arguments stand out, but for me the elephant in the room, so to speak, is the radical contrast between the 1644 confession and the 1689 confession concerning the doctrine of the law.

Jon Harley
Author of *Galatians and the New Covenant Theology Hermeneutic* and *Jesus, Son of Liberty: A New Covenant Theology Reply to the Doctrine of the Active Obedience of Christ.*

Introduction

Christians are a confessing people. From apostolic times, the saints have seen the importance of declaring what they believe about the Son of God. 1 Corinthians 15:3-8 stands as a creed of the faith; a written declaration of what God's people are to believe:

> *For I passed on to you as most important what I also received:*
>
> *that Christ died for our sins according to the Scriptures, that He was buried, that He was raised on the third day according to the Scriptures, and that He appeared to Cephas, then to the Twelve.*
>
> *Then He appeared to over 500 brothers at one time; most of them are still alive, but some have fallen asleep.*
>
> *Then He appeared to James, then to all the apostles.*
>
> *Last of all, as to one abnormally born, He also appeared to me.*

This reminds us that believing in the death and resurrection of Christ Jesus for the payment for our sins is the irreducible essence of what it means to believe on Him.

For several hundred years after the close of the canon of Scripture, God's people periodically wrote creeds and confessions to clarify their beliefs and refute error. See this author's book, *In Darkness – Light! The Millennium before the Reformation: How God preserved His people during the Dark Ages*; chapter 1, for a review of these documents.

1

Introduction

As time progressed, the growing papal empire tried to erase Christianity from the earth, but the people of God have a Defender Who cannot be defeated. During the Dark Ages, little was written by those being persecuted by Rome, but when the time was right, the printing press made it easier for people to produce their thoughts. Faith confessions started appearing in the late 16th century and in the 17th century, long confessions and systems of theology began to emerge. In our day, some appear to have concluded that man's growing in understanding the Scriptures came to an end in the 17th century, asking non-conformists if they know more than "the Westminster Divines" and so forth.

One 19th century author observed:

> The Confessions published by the Baptists in the Seventeenth Century were neither creeds written to secure uniformity of belief, nor articles to which subscription was demanded. They were rather expressions of their opinions, issued in this particular form, as being most convenient. They were defences, or Apologies (in the original senses of that term), wrung from them by the shameless calumnies and bitter misrepresentations of their enemies.[1]

The state-church of England had made life difficult for all who did not submit to their theology and rule. These confessions were a formal way to appeal to the government, explaining they were not a risk to the state religion or its political government.

It is wise to recall the words of Charles Spurgeon, in his endorsement of the 1689 London Baptist Confession in the preface he published for his people:

---

[1] J. Jackson Goadby, *Bye-Paths in Baptist History*, p. 106.

> This little volume, is not issued as an authoritative rule, or code of faith, whereby you are to be fettered, but as an assistance to you in controversy, a confirmation in faith, and a means of edification in righteousness. Here the younger members of our church will have a body of divinity in small compass, and by means of the scriptural proofs, will be ready to give a reason for the hope that is in them.

Spurgeon's words align with Goadby and ought to remind us not to revere these good and useful documents written by godly men to be anything more than aids to help us. They are not to be held as authoritative and binding, as if they were our rule of life.

Where to begin and what to include in this historical journey is quite subjective on my part. This is not a comprehensive, detailed review of everything concerning these documents; it is a selective overview intended to provide a good foundation for the reader to understand them. I will try to highlight the historical and theological context so the reader is not left with a merely factual review. Most everyone acknowledges that context is a most, if not the most, important rule in rightly comprehending literature. This rule holds just as surely for reading history, as viewing scenes detached from their context can lead to erroneous conclusions just as it can in literature. It is reckless to embrace and teach a confession as the rule of life without knowing the historical context of the confession – what caused the men to write it, what were their motives?

These two Baptist confessions were written and published by men living in the tedium of life unique to them – in their culture, period of history, and the theological development of their beliefs. While many books have been written by Baptists on the topic of confessions, the preponderance of those books are academic and biased towards the 1689 London Baptist Confession. My intention is to present a non-academic overview of how these confessions came to be, giving both confessions adequate light to see if they are true to the Bible so they will be used in the proper way.

> If we are serious about being people of the Book, we must be careful to keep our traditions and confessions in their rightful place –subordinate to the Word of God, not held up as an interpretative grid for God's Holy Scriptures. We must continue to grow in the grace and knowledge of our Lord (2 Peter 3:18), and the Scriptures are authoritative and sufficient for this.[2]

It is my prayer that the saints of the living God be people of the Book, His Scriptures, and not be merely devoted to a system of theology.

Many thanks to Rey Seveses and James Miller for editing the manuscript, making this book much better that I could do on my own.

Stuart L. Brogden   Author of *Captive to the Word of God, The Gospel In Isaiah, The Gospel In Romans, The End of All Things, and In Darkness – Light!* Also, the editor of Baptist Reprints.

P.S. While I use the commonly accepted term "paedobaptist" to refer to those who sprinkle babies and call it baptism, putting water on an infant or any unbeliever is not biblical water baptism. "Paedobaptism", then, is a euphemism and is not baptism in the New Covenant sense.

---

[2] Stuart L. Brogden, *Captive to the Word of God*, p. 132.

1. Development of the 1644 London Baptist Confession

There are many Particular Baptists[3] who hold to the 1646 version of the 1st London Baptist Confession (LBC), rather than the initial edition. For reasons I will reveal, this examination will be focused on the original 1644 edition.

The 1644 LBC opened with this disclaimer:

> A CONFESSION OF FAITH of seven congregations or churches of Christ in London, which are commonly, but unjustly, called Anabaptists; published for the vindication of the truth and information of the ignorant; likewise for the taking off those aspersions which are frequently, both in pulpit and print, unjustly cast upon them.

This rejection of Anabaptists has a historical context that cannot be ignored. As discussed below and detailed in **Appendix 1 – The Anabaptist Connection**, history reveals men interacted with people outside their own circle. William Lumpkin explains the context behind the statement in the 1644 LBC: "In 1535 Münster was seized by the Hoffmannites who, on being attacked, chose to defend themselves. A long siege followed, during which distorted tales of what was going on within the city were used to bring universal opprobrium upon the name Anabaptist. At length the city was reduced and the surviving defenders tortured and massacred. A year later, at Buckholt, Westphalia, Obbe Philips led a general meeting of the Anabaptists of Germany and the Netherlands. Most had had nothing to do with the Münster episode, and now they reiterated their non-resistant

---

[3] This term describes Baptists who hold the particular redemption of the elect only.

convictions."[4] The Anabaptists that these Baptists did not want to be confused with were those who tried to overthrow the government in Münster. Other sober-minded Anabaptists were not a risk and historical records show there was interaction and exchange of ideas with these brothers.

Like all confessions, the 1644 LBC was written by men who had been influenced by others; this impacted their beliefs and what they wrote. One confession that influenced the 1644 LBC was a paedobaptist document known as The True Confession. The 1644 LBC had 53 articles; the 1596 True Confession had 42. Twenty-nine articles of the 1596 are found in the 1644; not all are exactly the same, but they share a large degree of content and wording such that the correlation cannot be ignored. Yet, The True Confession is not the only source used by the authors of the 1644 LBC.

While many deny any outside influence on the development of the 1644 LBC, history is messy, comprised of people who ventured far and wide to discover what they considered truth. Again, Lumpkin is one who recognized the interaction among several groups that most historians keep separate. Lumpkin observed, "in its English manifestation, the Baptist Movement reflected, particularly, a heritage from an older native reform spirit as well as a heritage from sixteenth-century Continental Anabaptism and Calvinism."[5] He continued:

> Years afterward, even when organized life and witness were no longer possible, the spirit and distinctive emphases of Anabaptism survived on the English scene. Heath says, "The more the matter is studied, the more it will be seen that in its interest in

---

[4] William L. Lumpkin, *Baptist Confessions of Faith*, p.41-42.
[5] Ibid, p. 12.

Anabaptist teaching England was second only to Germany and the Netherlands."[6] It seems reasonable to suppose that, unconsciously or otherwise, principles of Anabaptism became a part of the thinking of zealous Englishman who were seeking a more thorough reformation of the Church in their land.[7]

Not a "pure stream of theology" worked out in isolation; the first generation particular Baptists were involved in a life and death struggle for their spiritual lives. The reality of saints who shared some doctrines was a great encouragement to these brethren who faced trials at every turn.

Thomas Helwys was a General Baptist who wrote a confession of faith in 1611. That confession had 27 articles, 8 of which had some correlation to content in the 1644 LBC. This correlation is not as direct or as close as those between the True Confession of 1596 and the 1644 LBC.

Similar points of emphasis and phrasing as contained in the 1644 LBC are found in Menno Simons' book, *A Foundation and Plain Instruction of the Saving Doctrine of Our Lord Jesus Christ*[8] (referred to *The Foundation Book*). This association is more fully explored in **Appendix 1 – The Anabaptist Connection.**

The correlation between these documents reveals an association, to some degree, between the men that wrote them. None of the 17th century confessions of faith were developed in isolation. Each was the product of men living in a culture quite different from ours – one that featured the

---

[6] Richard Heath, Contemporary Review, p. 176, 1895.
[7] Lumpkin, p. 14.
[8] Available from Brogden's Book at
https://www.amazon.com/dp/B08PZW77HQ

heavy hand of religious persecution and harassment from the state religion. Staying true one's conscience often made survival itself very difficult.

The editors of Backus Books Publishers, who reprinted the 1646 edition of the London Confession with Benjamin Cox's Appendix, offered this observation. "There are other baptistic statements of faith already available in our day, such as the Second London Confession of 1689, which is a modification of the Presbyterian Westminster Confession of Faith of 1646. Although these confessions agree on the fundamentals of Christian faith, there is a distinctive New Covenant emphasis concerning biblical law in the 1644 and 1646 editions of the First London Confession that is regretfully lacking in the Old Covenant emphasis of the Westminster and Second London Confessions. This difference has far reaching theological implications."[9]

A student at Southern Seminary read *Baptists Through the Centuries: A History of a Global People*, by David Bebbington, in which the case was made that the 1644 LBC was influenced by writings of Menno Simons – particularly in the common phrase, "death, burial, and resurrection" found in Simons' *Foundation of Christian Doctrine* and the 1644 LBC, in reference to water baptism. This student noted that this same phrase was also found in William Ames' *The Marrow of Theology* – "a popular work during the first half of the seventeenth-century and the Particular Baptist framers of the Confession were almost assuredly familiar with it."[10] He goes on to say, "While Simons clearly makes use of the "death, burial, and resurrection" motif in his section on baptism, this of itself does not suggest an intellectual

---

[9] Michael N. Ivey, *A Welsh Succession of Primitive Baptists*, p 26.
[10] Dustin Bruce, https://andrewfullercenter.org/media/blog/2013/03/the-intellectual-origins-of-the-1644-london-baptist-confession

influence upon the Particular Baptist framers of the 1644 document. The connection between Romans 6:3-5 and baptism was clearly made by Ames in his *The Marrow of Theology*, which even Stassen recognizes as influential upon the 1644 Confession." And he concludes by admitting, "it could be that the originators of the first Particular Baptist confession were not relying on either work, but thoughtfully reading their Greek New Testament."[11]

That excursion is but one example of how some Baptists are eager to disclaim any connection with Anabaptists in their zeal to claim a "pure" and "unsoiled" connection with the Puritans. William Ames was a paedobaptist and a few paragraphs after the citation mentioned above, he declares,

> But it appears the infants of the faithful are not to be forbidden this Sacrament, 1. Because if they are partakers of any grace, it is by virtue of the Covenant of Grace; and so both the covenant and the first seal of that covenant also pertain to them. 2. In that the covenant in which the faithful are now contained, is the same as that covenant which was made with Abraham, Rom 4.11; Gal 3.7-8; and that expressly extended to Infants. 3. This covenant which is now administered to the faithful, brings larger and fuller consolation to them than it could of old, before the coming of Christ. But if it were to pertain only to them, and not to their infants, then the grace of God and their consolation would be narrower and more contracted.[12]

---

[11] Dustin Bruce, https://andrewfullercenter.org/media/blog/2013/03/the-intellectual-origins-of-the-1644-london-baptist-confession.

[12] William Ames, *A Marrow of Theology*, page 210.

Why would the early Particular Baptists be inclined to use the paedobaptist Ames' language on one of the main topics of disagreement when Simons' view had the same theological foundation on water baptism they did? Would it not be dishonest to take part of what Ames wrote on baptism and ignore the larger context he wrote on the topic, then claim Ames' document as the source? Cherry picking, they call it.

Another confession which pre-dates the 1644 LBC and has some similar content is *The 1575 Confession of Faith by Two Baptist Martyrs*, written by Hendrik Terwoort and Jan Peters while in prison. These men were known as Anabaptists, rejected out-right by the state-church and the Magisterial Reformers in the Westminster, Savoy, and 1689 LBC companies. Possibly the only argument with this confession would be the position of taking no oaths (paragraph 12). This is simply another orthodox document which was available and possibly known by the men who wrote the 1st LBC, written by men who called themselves Baptist and believed much the same as what was laid down in the 1644 LBC.

Another group rejected out-right by most Calvinistic Baptists are the General Baptists, who believe that Christ died for everyone. Yet there are doctrines in common with this group as with Anabaptists. John Smyth was a well-known early General Baptist; he wrote a short confession in 1609, based on the Anabaptist Waterlander Confession of 1577. Regarding the Waterlander Confession, an Anabaptist historian observed it was the oldest theological formulation of that group and "it was meant to be a statement for the church, and was drawn up … by five leading ministers. This does not imply that a binding status was given to it. The Waterlanders would have been the first to reject this suggestion. They had arisen as a movement in large measure in protest against the rigor of church discipline among the Mennonites."[13] This is included to provide support to Goadby's statement regarding the purpose of these confessions, in the Introduction.

John Smyth's confession reflected discontinuity between the Old and New Covenants, between Law and Christ. We see this in Articles 10 & 11:

> In him is fulfilled, and by him is taken away, an intolerable burden of the law of Moses, even all the shadows and figures; as, namely, the priesthood, temple, altar, sacrifice; also the kingly office, kingdom, sword, revenge appointed by the law, battle and whatsoever was a figure of his person or office, so thereof a shadow or representation.
>
> And as the true promised Prophet he hath manifested and revealed unto us whatsoever God asketh or requireth of the people of the New Testament; for as God, by Moses and the other prophets, hath spoken and declared his will to the people of the Old Testament; so hath he in those last days, by his Prophet spoken unto us, and revealed unto us the mystery (concealed from the beginning of the world), and hath now manifested to us whatsoever yet remained to be manifested.[14]

William Roscoe Estep observed, "From these two articles, it is clear that the signers of this confession, which included Smyth, and the forty-one of those who had sought refuge

---

[13] Cornelius J. Dyck, Commentary,
https://www.anabaptistwiki.org/mediawiki/index.php?title=Waterlander _Confession_of_Faith_(1577).

[14] John Smyth, Short Confessions of Faith in XX Articles by John Smyth, in *Baptist Confessions of Faith* by William L. Lumpkin, p. 105.

with him in the Netherlands, held that the Mosaic Law was a burden, which Christ had removed and replaced. This much is evident in several articles in the confession but particularly in Article 21 which reads:"[15]

> Man being thus justified by faith, liveth and worketh by love (which the Holy Ghost sheddeth into the heart) in all good works, in the laws, precepts, ordinances given them by God through Christ; he praiseth and blesseth God, by a holy life, for every benefit, especially of the soul; and so are all such plants of the Lord trees of righteousness, who honor God through good works, and expect a blessed reward.[16]

From Estep: "In this confession it is clear that the law of Moses was replaced by Christ, who fulfilled the Law. It is also quite evident that as with most Anabaptists, the Old Testament no longer had the force of the New Testament for the Christian."[17]

Many current day theologians have seen the same perspective on the Law of Moses and Christ in the 1644 LBC. This is one reason Magisterial Reformers took issue with the 1st LBC and continue to do so today. This brings me to the reasons I do not endorse the 1646 version of the 1st LBC. First are changes made in response to criticism. Daniel Featley was briefly a member of the Westminster Assembly and a self-appointed "heresy-hunter". He criticized the 1644 LBC for several things, including speaking against state-paid ministers, advocating believer's baptism, and permitting non-ordained men to preach. In response to

---

[15] William Roscoe Estep, *Law And Gospel In The Anabaptist/Baptist Tradition*, p. 201.
[16] Lumpkin, p. 105.
[17] Estep, p 201.

Featley's criticism, the 1ˢᵗ LBC was revised; "In article 38, they dropped the language against state support of ministers. They even slightly altered their language on baptism to head off some of his carping."[18]

A close comparison of these two editions reveals the scope of change on these two topics:

1644	1646
That Baptism is an ordinance of the New Testament, given by Christ, to be dispensed only upon persons professing faith, or that are Disciples, or taught, who upon a profession of faith, ought to be baptized.	Baptism is an ordinance of the New Testament, given by Christ, to be dispensed upon persons professing faith, or that are made disciples; who upon profession of faith, ought to be baptized, and after to partake of the Lord's Supper.
That the due maintenance of the officers aforesaid, should be the free and voluntary communication of the Church, that according to Christ's ordinance, they that preach the Gospel, should live on the Gospel and not by constraint to be compelled from the people by a forced law.	The ministers of Christ ought to have whatsoever they shall need, supplied freely by the church, that according to Christ's ordinance they that preach the Gospel should live of the gospel by the law of Christ.

Baptism was added as a precursor to participating in the Lord's Supper, a long-standing position of Magisterial Reformers. While Scripture shows both ordinances for believers only, baptism as a prerequisite for the Lord's Supper is not specified therein.

---

[18] James Renihan, "Confessing The Faith In 1644 And 1689", p. 4.

The prohibition of tax-funded ministers was simply removed. James Renihan, a 1689 LBC advocate, summarized:

> The Baptists toned down or altered some of their language so that it would be more acceptable to the paedobaptists around them. Now I don't think that they were compromising. They were simply carrying out their original purpose. They wanted these men to acknowledge their orthodoxy, and understood that the only way to do this successfully was to reconsider some of their expressions. We must always remember this. The First London Confession of 1644 was an attempt to remove the threat of persecution and gain theological acceptance from paedobaptists, and the second edition of 1646 was even more explicitly so.[19]

My second reason for preferring the 1644 over the 1646 LBC is the addition of Benjamin Coxe's appendix defending particular redemption. This document doubled the length of the confession, making it – in my opinion – too long for use as a congregational doctrinal statement. The 1644 edition is clear enough on this topic for it to be recognized as a confession of advocating particular redemption; it is clearly not a general Baptist document. The 1646 LBC is often conflated with the 1644 LBC by 1689 LBC advocates who insist the 1st & 2nd LBCs are "substantially the same". By using the 1646 edition, the 1689 LBC advocates find a second signer in common – Hanserd Knollys. This adds to their argument to equality of content. This is a very weak argument, as we shall see in chapter 5.

---

[19] James Renihan, "Confessing The Faith In 1644 And 1689", p. 4.

Every child of God is prone to pragmatism, taking actions to gain a given response. I think Renihan doesn't see the movement described as compromise – they moved a bit closer to his doctrinal position. While we in 21st century USA can only imagine the persecution faced by these brothers, these changes were pragmatic. I am reminded of a convicting observation made long before I was born:

> Baptist growth has always been in proportion to the staunchness with which Baptist principles have been upheld and practised. So it ever has been with all religious bodies. Nothing is gained by smoothing off the edges of truth and toning down its colors, so that its contrast with error may be as slight as possible. On the contrary, let the edges remain a bit rough, let the colors be heightened, so that the world cannot possibly mistake the one for the other, and the prospect of the truth gaining acceptance, is greatly increased. The history of every religious denomination teaches the same lesson: progress depends on loyalty to truth. Compromise always means decay.[20]

Our basis for understanding the Bible must not be determined by the outcome we anticipate, but on the desire to know what the Lord has revealed to us. A hermeneutic that is founded on the response of man is flawed from the beginning. Our doctrines are not all essential, but they each and every one should reflect what the Creator of all things has actually spoken to us; for if we compromise on truth in a small thing, it will be "easier" to do so on something essential.

---

[20] Henry Vedders, *A Short History of the Baptists*, pages 110-111.

At the same time, we cannot impose our current state of political liberty onto those who lived in 17th century England. The following was written in commenting on pragmatic changes made during the drafting the of 2nd LBC, but it is directly relevant here:

> **We must not think harshly of these tortured brothers' willingness to seize this opportunity to gain official tolerance.** None today have lived under constant threat of imprisonment or worse for practicing their religion. None have seen their pastors drawn upon the rack and quartered. None have gone to their meeting house and found their pastor's head mounted on a pike in the church yard.[21]

Harsh circumstances do affect humans. So, let's disagree with a doctrine without condemning those who signed off on it.

Back to the development of the 1644 LBC, we return to Estep, who cites article XXV:

> That the tenders of the Gospel to the conversion of sinners, is absolutely free, no way requiring, as absolutely necessary, any qualifications, preparations, terrors of the Law, or preceding ministry of the Law, but only and alone the naked soul, as a sinner and ungodly to receive Christ, as Christ, as crucified, dead, and buried, and risen again, being made a Prince and a Savior for such sinners.

His conclusion: "This article intends to say that the Law, much as the General Baptists said, is a burden and a terror

---

[21] Michael N. Ivey, *A Welsh Succession of Primitive Baptist Faith and Practice*, p. 31.

from which the Christian is set free. But it goes on to imply that the purpose of the Law was to reveal the sinful soul, naked in the presence of God, and yet one that could receive Christ, and, therefore, experience new life in Him. This confession also acknowledges in Articles XXVIII and XXIX "Christ as head and King in this new Covenant" It is followed by the statement in Article XXX."[22]

> All believers through the knowledge of that justification of life given by the Father, and brought forth by the blood of Christ, have this as their great privilege of that New Covenant, peace with God, and reconciliation, whereby they that were afar off, were brought nigh by that blood, and have (as the Scripture speaks) peace passing all understanding, yes, joy in God, through our Lord Jesus Christ, by whom we have received the Atonement.

Again, from Estep: "It is evident from these articles that the Particular Baptists gave less attention to the Law and the Gospel than did the General Baptists. In spite of their Calvinistic soteriology, they too, identified the Old Covenant with the Law, which is no longer binding, and the New Covenant with Christ, who is the new "Lawgiver" who establishes his law in the heart."[23]

Estep reveals his view, that Anabaptists and General Baptists were odd-balls in regarding the Law of Moses as not binding on the saints, seeing Christ as a new law-giver "who establishes his law in the heart." Clearly this does not align with the Magisterial Reformers' view on Mosaic Law; but it does align with the revelation of Scripture!

---

[22] Estep, p. 203.
[23] Ibid.

Matthew Henry provides this insight, in his commentary on Exodus 7:20:

> let me observe in general concerning this plague that one of the first miracles Moses wrought was turning water into blood, but one of the first miracles our Lord Jesus wrought was turning water into wine; for the law was given by Moses, and it was a dispensation of death and terror; but grace and truth, which, like wine, make glad the heart, came by Jesus Christ.

When Jesus was introducing His kingdom, which is synonymous with the New Covenant, He said it could not even be seen – much less entered into – unless one was born from above (John 3:3). Paul expounded on the nature of this spiritual kingdom, in giving counsel for walking in brotherly love:

> *For if your brother is hurt by what you eat, you are no longer walking according to love. Do not destroy that one Christ died for by what you eat. Therefore, do not let your good be slandered, for the kingdom of God is not eating and drinking, but righteousness, peace, and joy in the Holy Spirit. Whoever serves Christ in this way is acceptable to God and approved by men.* (Romans 14:15-18)

The Mosaic Covenant community was mainly focused on behavior - "*Don't handle, don't taste, don't touch*" – so as to avoid the ritual pollution which required ritual cleansings, such as found in Leviticus 15 and 17. This was how the Mosaic Law operated, teaching people to live differently than the pagans lived. The law and its covenant were works-based; God treated national Israel with compassion and kindness for His name's sake, not because it was part of that covenant.

Rather than developing a system of theology built on "trans-covenantal law", the early Baptists realized the spiritual nature of the New Covenant which was shown as shadows and types by the Old Covenant (Hebrews 8). The common view with Anabaptists and General Baptists on this Biblical truth did not require accepting the system of soteriology held to by many in those camps; just as sharing the Calvinistic views of the Magisterial Reformers did not require accepting their view of covenants and law. It is a far better way of discerning the proper path than clinging wholly to any one system.

While we see influence of Anabaptist and General Baptist theology in the 1644 LBC, this confession is not intentionally copied from another document from another theological system. As we will see in chapter 3, the 1689 LBC is a self-described "step-child" of the Westminster Confession of Faith and the Savoy Declaration.

As a particular Baptist striving to be a man of the Book, I find much attachment to the 1644 LBC.

2. Summary of 1644 LBC Doctrine

The men who wrote the 1644 LBC aimed to declare their views on certain doctrines as an apologetic/defense of their beliefs as particular Baptists. This was a time of discovery and shaking out ideas that had been occupying the minds of saints for many years. Baptists were a new group, being first identified as such in 1609; but being identified by certain doctrines that had been clung to God's children since ancient times.

While examining the distinctives that mark people as Baptists, we must bear in mind that the label "Baptist" is secondary. Being true to biblical principles and precepts is essential. The label "Baptist" reflects who we are, it does not determine who we are. There are several doctrinal teachings Baptists have historically held that mark us as Baptist. Some divide these up into as many as eight points, but the essential Baptist distinctives can be summed up in the four categories examined below: 1.) Ordinances, 2.) The Nature of the Congregation, 3.) Liberty of Conscience, and 4.) View of Scripture. If we examine history, we will find children of God struggling to be true to convictions that reflect these same beliefs, even as the state-church (in several manifestations) sought to eliminate them from history.

A Baptist brother observed this tension-filled environment in early 17th century England:

> By the mid 1640s, Baptist practice was growing in London and the potential for persecution was ripe. A popular pamphlet, entitled "A Warning for England, especially for London; in the famous History of the frantick [sic] Anabaptists, their wild Preachings and Practices in Germany" was being distributed at the time. It charged the Baptist churches with being a

particular sect of "Anabaptism" that sought to sow seeds of governmental discord and perhaps even overthrow the government itself. Nothing could have been further from the truth, for in reality the Baptist churches of London wanted nothing to do with governmental matters; they simply wanted to be free to worship as they pleased.[24]

As noted in Chapter 1 – Development of the 1644 London Baptist Confession, there was some interaction among Anabaptists, General Baptists, and Particular Baptists as these three groups shared some of the essentials of what we now recognize as Baptist doctrines.

A reminder about the disclaimer in the 1644 LBC about being "falsely called Anabaptists":

> While we typically think of the Anabaptists as being more pacifistic in nature, there was a sect in Munster, Germany in the 1530s, who had sought to overthrow the local government. Having taken up arms, they took possession of the local court house and wanted to create their own civil authority. The uprising was squelched, but the fears sparked by this group continued for many years. It was the Anabaptists of Munster who inspired the pamphlet and flamed the fears of London in the 1640s.[25]

The influence of what I call "sober-minded Anabaptists" is reviewed in **Appendix 1 – The Anabaptist Connection**. Menno Simons is highlighted as being most influential in some of the content of the 1644 LBC. This was touched on in Chapter 1. Another Anabaptist who shared our view on

---

[24] Shane Kastler, "Comparing The Confessions: The History of the 1646 & 1689 London Baptist Confessions of Faith".
[25] Ibid.

ecclesiology was Jan Hus, who wrote an exposition on this, titled *De Ecclesia*[26].

The other group mentioned, General Baptist, contributed one of the most in-depth and earliest apologetics for liberty of conscience, printed in 1614.

> The Plea for liberty of Conscience is no new Doctrine, as old certainly as the blessed Word of God itself, which gives us this unmovable foundation. That every man should be fully persuaded of the truth of that way wherein he serves the Lord. And though there has been struggling in all ages to make good this blessed birthright to all peaceful people, yet through the Potency and subtlety of Popes, Bishops, and Ministers that preferred the advance of themselves, and their usurped and abused Function, before the good and welfare of the People, we have been deprived of this blessing. Next to the manifestation of God's love and goodness to us, the most excellent and desirable in this world: for want whereof, and by means of its contrary, persecution.[27]

As he makes clear in his introduction, his treatise was addressed to King James, and the Parliament, his main audience was "the Presbyterian reader."

> I hope, upon your reading thereof, you who are my Brethren of the Presbyterian way, will abandon much of your misguided eagerness in prosecuting your conscientious Brethren.[28]

---

[26] Available here: https://www.amazon.com/dp/B0C1JGPLK8
[27] Leonard Busher, *Religion's Peace*, p. 7.
[28] Ibid, p. 8.

Presbyterians and their forebearers had taken up the persecution of non-conformers they had learned from Rome. The early Presbyterian religion in England was a state-church and sought to re-establish that status after the King of England divorced himself from Rome and established the Anglican Church. The state-church always persecutes non-conformers. While Baptists share some beliefs with our Presbyterian brothers, it was much more difficult to have close association with them as long as they had the power of a state-church. There was much less risk to life and liberty in associating with sober-minded Anabaptists and General Baptists. This helps us understand the historical context and the reasons for such informal associations.

In the 1644 LBC, we see a defense of the Holy Trinity (articles I & II), Sovereignty of God (articles III & IV), and man's depravity (article V). The list goes on for 53 articles, all of which align with Baptist and Calvinistic doctrines, without the unnecessary baggage of the Presbyterian system of theology,

We find a substantial review of the office of our Lord Jesus in article X: "Jesus Christ only is made the Mediator of the New Covenant, even the everlasting covenant of grace between God and man, to be perfectly and fully the Prophet, Priest and King of the Church of God for evermore." Expansion of this idea runs through article XX.

As has been noted elsewhere in this work (chapter 1), the 1st LBC does not impose law as a precursor to the gospel. None but the Holy Spirit is seen as necessary or able to convert the soul at enmity with God. Article XXVI proclaims, "That the same power that converts to faith in Christ, the same power carries on the (1) soul still through all duties, temptations, conflicts, sufferings, and continually what ever a Christian is, he is by (2) grace, and by a constant renewed (3) operation from God, without which he cannot perform any duty to God, or undergo any temptations from Satan, the world, or men." No compromise with those who say man improves himself – nothing good done in or by us unless the Spirit works it.

Union with Christ is highlighted in article XXVIII: "those which have union with Christ, are justified from all their sins, past, present," The trouble we are certain to have in this world is reviewed in articles XXXI and XXXII, the latter confirms that "Jesus Christ, who is the Captain of their salvation" is the only One who can uphold and protect them during the on-going conflict we will have with this world.

The ecclesiology of this confession is detailed in articles XXXIII – XXXVI, showing each local congregation as part of His spiritual kingdom in this age, led and commanded only by our Chief Shepherd and King; no ecclesiastical hierarchy as clung to by the state-church mindset that even today besets far too many Christians. In the Baptist view, the local assembly is an expression of the complete body of Christ, which is comprised of all the redeemed. There is no human authority that unites us as brethren. This opposition to a state-church is why the 1644 LBC says (article XXXVIII) that elders are to be paid by the people they serve and "not by constraint to be compelled from the people by a forced law." Taxes are how the state-church is funded, following the theocracy God established with national Israel – not with any Christian organization.

Baptism, discipline, and service are found in articles XXXIX – XLVII. This last-mentioned article stresses unity in the local assembly and an "other" focus in service. "And although the particular congregation be distinct and several bodies, every one a compact and knit city in itself; yet are they all to walk by one and the same Rule, and by all means convenient to have the counsel and help one of another in all needful affairs of the church, as members of one body in the common faith under Christ their only Head."

Articles XLIV – L review the Baptist view of civil Magistrates, advising "that all lawful things commanded by them, subjection ought to be given by us in the Lord. … although we should suffer never so much from them in not actively submitting to some ecclesiastical laws, which might be conceived by them to be their duties to establish which we for the present could not see, nor our consciences could submit unto; yet are we bound to yield our persons to their pleasures." Further, "And if God should provide such a mercy for us, as to incline the magistrates' hearts so far to tender our consciences, as that we might be protected by them from wrong, injury, oppression and molestation, which long we formerly have groaned under by the tyranny and oppression of the Prelatical Hierarchy." Basically, we are to submit to civil authorities when it does not require us to go against the clear teachings of Scripture, but not when they require us to disobey Him, forbid us from obedience to Him, or go against conscience.

Articles LI – LIII review the tension in our lives, as we live as sojourners in this world, as children of the most high God. We are to continue in our Christian communion with one another regardless of what the state tells us, "not daring to give place to suspend our practice, but to walk in obedience to Christ in the profession and holding forth this faith before mentioned, even in the midst of all trails and afflictions. … remembering always we ought to obey God rather than men, and grounding upon the commandment, commission, and promise of our Lord and Master Jesus Christ, who as He has power in heaven and earth, so also has promised, if we keep His commandments which He has given us, to be with us to the end of the world." We are further admonished "to submit to the magistrate in the Lord, and the magistrate every way to be acknowledged, reverenced, and obeyed, according to godliness; not because of wrath only but for conscience sake … to give God that which is God's, and unto Ceasor that which is Ceasor's, and unto all men that which belongs unto them, endeavoring ourselves to have always a clear conscience void of offense towards God, and towards man."

The conclusion penned by these brothers includes this exhortation: "But if any man shall impose upon us anything that we see not to be commanded by our Lord Jesus Christ, we should, in His strength, rather embrace all reproaches and tortures of men, to be stript of all outward comforts, and if it were possible, to die a thousand deaths, rather than to do anything against the least tittle of the truth of God, or against the light of our own consciences."

I think it is hard for us, in the comfort of our 21st century homes, to grasp the mindset of these men and those Anabaptists who preceded them – willing to lose all earthly things rather than "do anything against the least tittle of the truth of God, or against the light of our own consciences." I dare say our lives are too much dictated by our desire for comfort than obedience. May God have mercy on us!

One of the things I like about the 1644 LBC is its concise nature. No need for a 300-page exposition to explain what it means. This confession can be understood by anyone indwelt by the Spirit, providing a sound foundation for congregational life as ordered by Him.

Some have complained that the 1644 LBC appears to have its content thrown together without topical arrangement. I have attempted to remedy this by providing a topically arranged edition of the 1644 LBC, with updated English for the 21st century reader. [29]

For those who say the 1644 LBC fails to address critical doctrines, I am willing to listen but am leery of adding too much, for with many words come opportunity for error and disagreement. In the 1644 LBC that I published, I added the following:

The Lord's Supper

Article 48. The Lord's Supper an Ordinance of the New Covenant, given by Christ, to be administered only to persons professing faith, are Disciples who spiritually receive, and feed upon Christ crucified, with all the benefits of His death; the body and blood of Christ being then not corporally or carnally, but spiritually present to the faith of believers. Ignorant and ungodly persons, as they are unfit to enjoy communion with Christ, so are they unworthy of the Lord's table, and cannot, without great sin against Him, while they remain such, partake of these holy mysteries, or be admitted thereunto. Yea, whosoever shall receive unworthily, are guilty of the body and blood of the Lord, eating and drinking judgment to themselves.

1 Cor. 11:23-26; 1 Cor. 10:16,17,21; 2 Cor. 6:14,15; 1 Cor. 11:29; Matt. 7:6.

Article 49. The reason this ordinance was given to the church is to declare the death of Christ; that He did die for the sins of His people; to demonstrate the manner of His death, by crucifixion; by his being

---

[29] This reprint can be found here:
https://www.amazon.com/dp/B0875SRH42

pierced, wounded, bruised, and broken; and to express the blessings and benefits of his death, and the faith of his people in Him, and thankfulness for His obedience. Further, we proclaim His death until returns; this reminds us that Jesus has gone to prepare a place for us and has promised to return to take us to be with Himself for eternity.

Heb. 10:12-14; John 1:29; John 14:3[30]

---

[30] Brogden, *The First London Baptist Confession of Faith*, p. 36-37.

Summary of 1644 LBC Doctrine

3. Development of the 1689 London Baptist Confession

The historical context of the 2nd London Baptist Confession is critical in understanding the content of that document. The middle of the 17th century in England was that of near chaos, as the King's state-church sought to dictate conscience and practice of all who claimed Christ. Political chaos also ruled the day, as civil war erupted in 1642 between supporters of King Charles I (an advocate of supreme, divine rule) and those who favored a constitutional monarchy. Oliver Cromwell was in this latter group and quickly rose to lieutenant-general in 1645.

After a few years of peace, civil war broke out again, in 1648, resulting in the execution of King Charles I in 1649, the elevation of Cromwell to Lord Protector in 1653, and the rise of the Fifth Monarchy[31]. This was a group of men from all religious camps that believed the fifth monarchy alluded to the second chapter of Daniel, following the Assyrian, Persian, Greek, and Roman monarchies; during which Christ should reign on earth with his saints for 1,000 years. This was hauntingly similar to the Münster rebellion of 1535, which sought to establish the "New Jerusalem" in Germany. The Fifth Monarchy failed, Oliver Cromwell died, and, in 1661, King Charles II was seated with a new, loyal parliament.

During Cromwell's reign, religious liberty continued to be a difficult thing to hold on to.

> As Cromwell's administration grew in bureaucracy, it became increasingly autocratic. This was

---

[31] Louis Brown's *Baptists and the Fifth Monarchy*, available at https://www.amazon.com/dp/B09L4Q5CBM

particularly the case in matters of religion, where despite a reformation of the Church of England which placed Presbyterian clergy at its head, an appetite for complete religious conformity still gnawed at the leadership. Fresh outbreaks of religious persecution occurred against the Baptists by these Calvinist brethren who now controlled the Church of England. According to James Tull the newly empowered Presbyterians held precisely the same views as their Anglican counterparts concerning religious conformity. "The Presbyterians intended for the church to be a national church, embracing the whole population in its membership. Dissent was not to be allowed; membership was compulsory. Everyone was to have his children baptized and to pay tithes. On this point there was to be little difference from the church as already established."[32]

Difficulty continued under Charles II and his parliament:

In 1662 The Act of Uniformity was passed. This act required use of the Anglican Book of Common Prayer in all religious meetings under penalty of loss of position … fines and/or imprisonment … because the book was essentially Catholic Episcopalian … approximately two thousand Anglican bishops left the Established Order and joined nonconforming congregations. Second, fines and imprisonments were systematically imposed upon non-conforming violators.

The Uniformity Act was quickly followed by other means of legislated persecution which included

---

[32] Ivey, p. 27-28.

reinstitution of The Conventicle Act in 1664. This law forbade nonconformist religious gatherings of more than four persons over the age of sixteen. Next, the Five-mile Act was passed in 1665. It prohibited nonconforming ministers from preaching within five miles of any city or village which sent members to Parliament or which had an Established Church within its boundaries. It also denied dissenters the right to teach in any public or private schools. In 1670 another Conventicle Act was passed. While this law did not carry a death penalty for repeat offenders, as did the original Conventicle Act, it was particularly cruel in that it allowed the Crown to seize all property of repeat offenders. Also, this law was very effective because it allowed informers to keep one third of everything seized. The second Conventicle Act was followed by the Test Act of 1673. This law barred nonconformist from holding civil or military office. The Test Act was followed by The Clarendon Code, which renewed the severest forms of persecution.

The tyranny of these laws resulted in fines, public beatings, imprisonment, and capital execution for dissenters. Offenders where often tortured to death. Executions were carried out by hanging, beating, beheading, impaling, dismembering, and burning. It is estimated that the malicious treatment of non-conformers (of which Baptists suffered more than any others owing to their public support of principles of religious liberty) resulted in persecution of more than seventy-thousand saints, of whom eight thousand perished. The sum total of fines levied and collected is calculated to be in excess of two-million pounds sterling, as calculated in 1850.

It was amid this climate of religious persecution that a small window of liberty briefly opened. In 1689, with the ascension of William and Mary to the throne, a new Act of Toleration was passed.[33]

I remind you of Michael Ivey's wise counsel: **We must not think harshly of these tortured brothers' willingness to seize this opportunity to gain official tolerance.**[34]

Although first composed in 1677 while under persecution from the Church of England, the 1689 Second London Baptist Confession was published, with names attached, four months after the 1689 Act of Toleration granted by William and Mary of Orange. The Toleration Act, (May 24, 1689), act of Parliament granted freedom of worship to Nonconformists (i.e., dissenting Protestants such as Baptists and Congregationalists).[35]

> By 1688, when the call went out for a Particular Baptist General Convention, the political climate in England had changed several times. During the forty-four years separating the adoption of the two Particular Baptist Confessions, a civil war occurred, a King was executed, democratic process was instituted and derailed, the Anglican church underwent reformation and a new King was crowned. Also, the cause of religious freedom suffered setbacks resulting in a systematic and legislated policy which is best described as an almost perpetual increase in intensity of persecution of dissenters.[36]

---

[33] Ivey, p. 28-29.
[34] Ibid, p.31.
[35] Britanica, Toleration Act.
[36] Ivey, p 26.

The 2nd London Baptist Confession was mostly based on the Westminster Confession of Faith (WCF) and the Savoy Declaration (SD, written by congregational paedobaptists), with little content from the 1644 LBC, and some original content.

Embracing these two paedobaptist congregations was not shown only in the finished work of the 1689 LBC authors, they made it publicly known in the introduction. From the Introduction to the 1689 LBC, on the Covenant Reformed Baptist Church website:

> To the Judicious and Impartial Reader:
>
> And forasmuch as our method, and manner of expressing our sentiments, in this, doth vary from the former (although the substance of the matter is the same) we shall freely impart to you the reason and occasion thereof. **One thing that greatly prevailed with us to undertake this work,** was (not only to give a full account of ourselves, to those Christians that differ from us about the subject of Baptism, but also) the profit that might from thence arise, unto those that have any account of our labors, in their instruction, and establishment in the great truths of the Gospel; in the clear understanding, and steady belief of which, our comfortable walking with God, and fruitfulness before him, in all our ways, is most nearly concerned; and therefore **we did conclude it necessary to express ourselves the more fully, and distinctly**; and also to fix on such a method as might be most comprehensive of those things which we designed to explain our sense, and belief of; and **finding no defect, in this regard, in that fixed on by the assembly, and after them by those of the Congregational way**, we did readily conclude it best

to retain the same order in our present confession: and also, when we observed that those last mentioned, did in their confession (for reasons which seemed of weight both to themselves and others) **choose not only to express their mind in words concurrent with the former in sense, concerning all those articles wherein they were agreed, but also for the most part without any variation of the terms** we did in like manner conclude it best to follow their example in making use of the very same words with them both, **in these articles (which are very many) wherein our faith and doctrine is the same with theirs**, and this we did, the more abundantly, to manifest our consent with both, in all the fundamental articles of the Christian Religion, as also with many others, whose orthodox confessions have been published to the world; on behalf of the Protestants in diverse Nations and Cities: and also to convince all, that we have no itch to clog Religion with new words, but do readily acquiesce in that form of sound words, which hath been, in consent with the holy Scriptures, used by others before us; hereby declaring before God, Angels, & Men, our hearty agreement with them, in that wholesome Protestant Doctrine, which with so clear evidence of Scriptures they have asserted: some things indeed, are in some places added, some terms omitted, and some few changed, but these alterations are of that nature, as that we need not doubt, any charge or suspicion of unsoundness in the faith, from any of our brethren upon the account of them. [37]

(emphasis and modernized English are mine)

---

[37] https://www.the1689confession.com/1689/introduction

To highlight one aspect of what the paragraph tells us, I've taken the highlighted statements and made a short paragraph, with a couple of notes:

> One thing that greatly prevailed with us to undertake this work, we did conclude it necessary to express ourselves the more fully, and **distinctly finding no defect** in that fixed on by the assembly *(the Westminster assembly)*, and after them by those of the Congregational way *(the Savoy Declaration)*, choose not only to express their mind in words concurrent with the former in sense, concerning all those articles wherein they were agreed, but also for the most part without any variation of the terms in these articles (which are very many) wherein **our faith and doctrine is the same with theirs**.

While some content in the 1689 LBC is taken from the 1644 LBC (the introduction does endorse it), the bulk of content is from the WCF and Savoy Declaration.

Using the comparison chart by James N. Anderson, I have counted 160 numbered paragraphs in the 32 chapters of the 1689 LBC. [38] I reviewed the content of these in comparison to the WCF and the SD to see where there was substantial agreement between the 1689 LBC and either or both of these. All three confessions are in agreement in 110 of the 160 paragraphs; the WCF and 1689 LBC agreed but not the SD in 3 paragraphs; the SD and the 1689 LBC agreed but not the WCF in 17 paragraphs. The 130 paragraphs that agree constitute 81% agreement between the 1689 LBC and these two paedobaptist confessions. The topics on which

---

[38] James N. Anderson, "A Tabular Comparison of the 1646 Westminster Confession of Faith, the 1658 Savoy Declaration of Faith, the 1677/1689 London Baptist Confession of Faith and the 1742 Philadelphia Confession of Faith".

there is the least agreement are chapters 26 – 30; on the church, communion of the saints, ordinances, baptism, laying on of hands, and the Lord's Supper.

Comparing the 1644 LBC with the 1689 LBC in a similar fashion is more difficult. The overall structure of the 1689 LBC follows the WCF to a large degree; the phrasing of many paragraphs is very close between them. These two things are not true between the two Baptist documents. The 1644 LBC has only 53 articles (paragraphs). It does not cover as many topics as the later confessions. The 1644 LBC does not have content correlating to chapters 5, 7, 9, 10, 12, 16 – 23, 25, 27, 28, and 30 – 32 of the 1689 LBC. The 2nd LBC does not have correlation to the content of ten articles (#13, 18-20, 33, 35, 44, 51-53) of the 1st LBC.

Where the 1st LBC agrees with the 2nd LBC there is virtually no phrasing in common. There are 13 topics, found in 43 articles of the 1644 LBC, where these 2 Baptist documents partially agree. As there is not complete alignment, nor do the common topics have similar lengths, it is not easy to say how many paragraphs are common. I have estimated that there are roughly 7 paragraphs of content that align. This amounts to 13% of the 1644 LBC being shared by the 1689 LBC. Of the 160 paragraphs of the 1689 LBC, the 7 equivalent paragraphs of the 1644 LBC account for 4% of the 1689 LBC.

I fail to understand how many 1689 LBC advocates claim these two covenants are substantially the same. The differences in these shared articles shows substantial lack of agreement. The 1644 LBC is much more focused on the multi-faceted roles of Christ Jesus: prophet, priest, king, mediator; the 1689 LBC focuses on Him as mediator.

Additionally, the 1689 LBC has 18 complete chapters and 114 paragraphs that have no correlation to the 1644 LCB. Many of these are topics the 1644 LBC simply does not address and do not represent disagreement; marriage and the Lord's Supper are examples.

> For reasons not entirely made clear, the London brethren did not use their 1644 Confession as a model for the 1689 document. Their stated reasons were its poor circulation among the Baptists and a general lack of familiarity with this earlier document among the attendants of the convention. However, their stated reason seems a bit strange since the first Confession underwent five printings in three editions and was distributed throughout England, Wales and Scotland.[39]

> The Baptists, yet suffering terribly at the hand of the Crown, eventually realized that neither the Presbyterians nor Congregationalists were suffering the same frequency and intensity of torment. Perhaps fully understanding the political reality of their circumstance they assembled in 1689 in a General Convention and officially adopted Collin's very Westminsterish confession.[40]

> The Confession itself was first compiled by the Elders and Brethren of many congregations of Christians, baptized upon their profession of faith, in London and the country (as they then described themselves) in the year 1677. It was based upon, and drew its inspiration from the Confession drawn up by the Westminster Assembly of Divines a generation earlier, and indeed

---

[39] Ivey, p. 29.
[40] Ivey, p. 30.

differs only from it in its teaching upon those matters, such as baptism, the Lord's Supper, and church government, upon which among the Reformed churches the Baptists differ from the Presbyterians. For fear of persecution, the compilers of the 1677 Confession did not subscribe their names to it, but when, in September, 1689, following the Revolution of the previous year, the Ministers and Messengers of the churches were able to meet in more peaceful times, thirty-seven of them, including all the most eminent Baptist ministers of the day, set their names to the recommendation with which it was circulated among the churches.[41]

Before the assembly convened, William Collins, a pastor in London, had revised the Westminster Confession to express a distinctive Baptist ecclesiology. With some exceptions, the proposed revision was in many places word for word identical with the Westminster document. Therefore, for the first time in any Baptist confession, there is a long section (Chapter 19) devoted to the Law of God.[42]

It states, "Neither doth Christ in the Gospel any way dissolve, but much strengthen this obligation." In the sixth paragraph it explains that this does not mean that we who know Christ are under a covenant of works, but nevertheless the law provides "a Rule of life, informing them of the Will of God, and their Duty, it directs and binds them, to walk accordingly discovering also the sinfull pollutions of their Natures, Hearts and Lives."[43]

---

[41] Steve Clevenger, Foreword to the 1689 London Baptist Confession.
[42] Estep, *Law and Gospel*, p. 204.
[43] Ibid, p. 205.

Absent from this confession and the Westminster Confession, is any emphasis upon "the burden," or "curse" of the law and the pedagogical function of the law in bringing one to Christ. The emphasis is, however, upon the Moral Law as enunciated by Moses in the decalogue which was held to be still binding upon the Christian, but not necessary for salvation. It appears that the Westminster Confession of Faith attempted to avoid the charge of antinomianism, while maintaining that salvation does not come through works but by grace. The Second London Confession, therefore, represents a greater shift from both the First London Confession of 1644 and 1646 than from the General Baptist Confession of 1612.[44]

The tedium of being spied on, arrested, imprisoned, executed; that was the Baptists' lot in the mid-17th century in England. It cannot fail to impact those who were suffering. It would be wrong to assert that the entire effort of writing and publishing the 2nd LBC was due to political, pragmatic reasons. It would be just as wrong to say that none of the work and decisions that went into this confession were influenced by political, pragmatic reasons.

The desire on the part of many Non-Conformists was to show unity with one another against the Church of England. Indeed, these various Calvinistic fellowships shared much in common doctrinally, while differing on other non-salvific issues. … From a political perspective, adoption of the 1689 Confession helped to unite the Non-Conformists against the attacks of the established religious power of the day, the Church of England. Yet the sometimes

---

[44] Estep, *Law and Gospel*, p. 205.

uncomfortable reality for those Baptists who hold to the 1689 Confession still stands: the document was largely adopted for political rather than theological purposes.[45]

We can likely agree that the optimum response to the risk of life and property would be as Polycarp's when he was arrested and sentenced to a horrible death:

> At sight of him, the mob sets up loud cries of rage and savage delight, but Polycarp hears a voice telling him, "Be strong and play the man!" Consequently, he does not allow the spite of the crowd to trouble him. The governor asks him to deny Christ and promises that if he will, his life will be spared. But the faithful bishop answers, **"Fourscore and six years have I served him, and he has never done me injury; how then can I now blaspheme my King and savior?"**[46]

But men with wives and children have dual responsibilities that are honorable (1 Cor. 7:33) and we cannot sit in judgment on these 17th century brothers, even if we disagree with some of their published doctrines.

I turn your attention to a current-day advocate of the 1689 LBC to check my understanding of the influences that were at work in its development. Samuel Renihan is the son of James Renihan; has an MDiv from Westminster Seminary California & Institute of Reformed Baptist Studies, PhD, Free University of Amsterdam; and is pastor of Trinity Reformed Baptist Church in La Mirada, California.[47]

---

[45] Kastler, "Comparing The Confessions: The History of the 1646 & 1689 London Baptist Confessions of Faith", Part One.
[46] Christian History Institute, Article 7.
[47] Founders Ministries, Authors Page.

The title of Renihan's book gives away his bias. *From Shadow to Substance, the Federal Theology of the English Particular Baptists (1642-1704)* implies a type-antitype relationship between the first and second London Baptist confessions, leaving the impression that the 1st LBC was good but incomplete and the 2nd LBC is both.

All of the men Renihan quoted from in chapter 2, Unity and Diversity in Reformed Covenant Theology, for the period from 1504 – 1640, are paedobaptists which, he says, were the foundation for the views developed and published by particular Baptists. There is an absence of the influence different groups had upon one another in these early days, when men were searching out how to document what they believed. General and particular Baptists rubbed against each other and some moved between the groups. Similar circumstances involved some who were called Anabaptist. History is not a surgically ordered line of thought that moved towards the historian's vision; history is messy, made up of men and women who did not have their theology all figured out and polished. The preface to the 1689 LBC confirms that it was based on and agreed with the doctrine of the Westminster Confession and the Savoy Declaration. The 1644 LBC, written and signed by first generation particular Baptists, makes no such admission. It seems Renihan is focused on establishing the paedobaptist community as the foundation for all Particular Baptists.

"Particular Baptist origin must be considered from a broad and narrow perspective. Broadly, their origins lie in the Puritan movement in the universities and parish churches of England. Narrowly, their origins lie in the emergence of John

Spilsbury's congregation from the so-called Jacob/Lathrop/Jessey church."[48]

"A proper understanding of the Particular Baptists' identity must consider the context of their origins in the Separatist wing of the Puritan movement of the church of England."[49]

"While confident in their doctrinal distinctives, the Particular Baptists were eager to establish their legitimacy among Presbyterians and Independents and at the same time to distance themselves from Arminians, Socinians, and Anabaptists. ... All that an opponent of the Baptists had to say was the name 'Munster', and all of the supposed horrors of that sad city would be imputed to their English 'counterparts'. The Particular Baptists' confession of faith was an attempt to vindicate their name in the eyes of the orthodox."[50] This is an admission that these Baptists saw the state-church of their day as orthodox and that the reason for their confession was to "vindicate their name in the eyes" of the state-church. From the pens of two generations of Particular Baptists, it would seem Renihan's observation is true of the second, but not the first.

Summing up a quote from Heinrich Bullinger: "God gave Adam a law, suspended a reward upon obedience to that law, provided a visible sign (sacrament) to fortify the commitment and relationship between them."[51]

Summing up a quote from John Calvin on the "covenant of law" and "the covenant of the gospel": "He then proceeded to reaffirm that they did not differ in substance, but rather in

---

[48] Samuel Renihan, p. 5.
[49] Ibid, p. 10.
[50] Ibid.
[51] Ibid, p. 17-18.

outward accidental differences."[52] (Note: for reasons unknown to me, Reformers use the term "accidental" where "administrative" is meant. Since they do claim one Covenant of Grace with two administrations, not accidents, it would make sense if they used "administrative" instead of "accidental". But they don't.)

Summing up Zacharias Ursinus: "He stated that "the law contains the covenant of nature (*foedus naturale*), which was made by God with man in creation." This covenant is known by nature, demands perfect obedience, and promises eternal life. ... Ursinus' clear use of the law and the gospel **dogmatically** and historically is enhanced by his identification of the law as a covenant, and as a covenant present at creation. What naturally followed from Ursinus' identification of the moral law as containing the covenant of nature, was that this covenant was repeated (*repetivit et declaravit*) at Mt. Sinai in the Ten Commandments. This means that the law and the gospel, **dogmatically**, were both present in the law and the gospel, historically. But in the time of the law, historically, the law, **dogmatically**, held a more prominent place, relatively speaking."[53] (emphasis mine) Ursinus dogmatically believed "the covenant of nature" contained "the law" – "the Ten Commandments" – even though the Bible says that law was not given until Mt. Horeb:

> Deuteronomy 5:1-3 *Moses summoned all Israel and said to them, "Israel, listen to the statutes and ordinances I am proclaiming as you hear them today. Learn and follow them carefully. The LORD our God made a covenant with us at Horeb. He did not make*

---

[52] Samuel Renihan, p. 19.
[53] Ibid, p. 25.

this covenant with our fathers, but with all of us who are alive here today.

This is right before Moses delivers the Decalogue to the people of Israel – not to the world.

But Renihan is dogmatic about it – in his own words. The Cambridge English Dictionary's definition of "dogmatic" contains this example: "The more dogmatically certain someone is, the further they are likely to be from enlightenment."

"For Olevianus, the *foedus legale* was made with Israel and revived the *foedus naturale* made with Adam."[54] Deuteronomy 5:1-5 makes it clear that the legal covenant which formed the Hebrew nation was not given to anyone other than that nation – not even the Patriarchs, much less Adam; it was given to those who were at the mountain and alive on the day when Moses spoke to them. It did not "revive" anything that had been given to Adam, coming nearly 1,500 years after Adam's death. There is nothing in the Bible indicating anything like the Mosaic Covenant was given to Adam. He was given a few commands: name the animals, rule over nature, don't eat from that one tree. Revelation is progressive, with God giving us more clarity over time. It is retrograde to project later Scripture back on earlier people as if it had been given to them. We can see the shadows in ancient time and we now know to what they pointed – all is fulfilled in the Lord Jesus.

"In fact, from the same passage, Galatians 4, Olevianus pointed out that the law, considered as the old covenant, or old administration of the covenant of grace, did indeed save sinners insofar as they looked to the promise or doctrine of

---

[54] Samuel Renihan, p. 26.

Christ as it was then revealed."[55] No covenant, no law saves sinners. Faith in the promised Seed did save some in the Old Covenant; the covenant did not save them, no law saved them. A preacher can point people to Christ, but he doesn't save them in doing so. Salvation is of the Lord, not of man nor of law nor of covenant.

> The spread of the Reformation from the continent to England, the succession of English rulers, and the increasing availability of literature produced an ever-shifting political, sociological, and theological environment. Within this context, a "Puritan" movement sought to reform the Church of England and bring its credenda and agenda into line with the Scriptures, abandoning what the Puritans considered to be the traditions of men. In this context of dissent and separation, the Particular Baptists emerged not just from the Church of England, but more specifically from semi-separatist Independents. Thus, when the Particular Baptists applied their Puritan zeal to infant baptism they were reforming themselves first and foremost, and then calling the larger English church to remove what they saw as unreformed tradition.[56]

Is there any doubt that Renihan seeks to prove an exclusive connection to the paedobaptists for Particular Baptists? This is the consistent bias of those who advocate the 1689 LBC. And that is why I added the reference to the Westminster Confession of Faith the graphic of the Founder's t-shirt.

---

[55] Samuel Renihan, p. 27.
[56] Ibid, p. 53.

4. Summary of 1689 LBC Doctrine

One well-known resource on the 1689 LBC is Sam Waldron's *Modern Exposition of 1689 Baptist Confession of Faith*. I will review parts of this confession and Waldron's exposition in order to determine if this document presents a cogent explanation of certain Christian doctrines.

Let me say at the outset that I think most of the content of the 1689 LBC is true and useful. My reason for reviewing this book is not to pick it apart as though every bit of it is suspect or the whole thing worthy of being discarded. Two reasons for this review: First, with many words comes increased opportunity for error; second, many 1689 advocates assert a theological heritage narrowly aligned with the Puritans, declaiming any connection to those called Anabaptist. I want to show how both of these problems are evident in Waldron's exposition and Samuel Renihan's book.

Waldron's exposition, from Chapter 2, paragraph 3: "In this divine and infinite Being there are **three subsistences**, the Father, the Word or Son, and Holy Spirit, **of one substance**, power, and eternity, each having the whole divine essence, yet the essence undivided: the **Father is of none, neither begotten nor proceeding; the Son is eternally begotten of the Father; the Holy Spirit proceeding from the Father and the Son**; all infinite, without beginning, therefore but one God, who is not to be divided in nature and being, but distinguished by several peculiar relative properties and personal relations; which doctrine of the Trinity is the foundation of all our communion with God, and comfortable dependence on Him." (emphasis mine)

The 1689 LBC says the Trinity is made of "three subsistences" that are "of one substance." Huh? Substistence is defined as "real being: existence, the condition of remaining in existence; means of subsisting." Substance means, "a particular kind of matter with uniform properties; the real physical matter of which a person or thing consists." An online philosophical dictionary reported: "Subsistence, Substance. The former of these words is derived from the verb subsisto, which among its shades of meaning signifies to remain. A thing subsistens per se is therefore something which has endurance in itself. Substance is derived by St. Augustine from the same verb; but by the majority from substo, to stand under. ... There would seem, therefore, to be no great difference between the meanings of the words subsistence and substance."[57] It is beyond me how one can say the Trinity is comprised of three subsistences that are of one substance instead of three persons who are each fully God, distinct but in perfect harmony as the Holy Trinity.

The 1689 LBC goes on to say, rather than the Son and Spirit are eternally such and are self-existent as is the Father, that the Son is "eternally begotten" and the Spirit eternally "proceeding" – as if they had no substances apart from those actions. The Son was "begotten" as a man in the fulness of time, not from eternity; the Spirit was sent by the Father and the Son in the fullness of time, not from eternity. These two momentous events were not needed until creation brought about the presence of man and the doom of sin.

*And we bring you the good news that what God promised to the fathers, this he has fulfilled to us their children by raising Jesus, as also it is written in the second Psalm, "'**You are my Son, today I have begotten you.**' (Acts 13:32-33 ESV)* By saying, *today I have begotten you*, Scripture puts a time-stamp on the event; it did not take place in "eternity past."

---

[57] PHILOSOPHICAL DICTIONARY – Subsistence, Substance.

The Greek word behind "begotten", as used in Acts 13:33, is
G1080 γεννάω gennao (ĕen-naō') v.
    1. (properly, of the father) to procreate.
    2. (by extension, of the mother) to conceive.
    3. (figuratively) to regenerate.[58]

How can an eternally self-existent being be "begotten"?

Waldron expounds: "The historic doctrine of the church and
its creeds is that as to their essence the Son and Spirit are
equal in power and glory to the father, but as to their persons
they are eternally generated and eternally proceed from the
Father. Thus, as to their essence, they are self-existent, while
as to their persons, they are eternally derived from the
Father."[59] Since the Son and the Spirit are each fully God,
they were not derived from the Father – to say they are puts
the Father as the source of the other two members of the
Trinity. The person and the essence of God cannot be
separated as though they exist independent of each other.
Each person is eternally self-existent, not derived.

"Without eternal generation and eternal procession and the
doctrine of hypostatic union it is impossible to distinguish
the different persons in the Trinity."[60] I fail to understand
how generation must be eternal in order to distinguish the
different persons in the Trinity. Jesus has always been God
the Son; He was generated as a man in time. That's when the
hypostatic union came into being. God the Son put on flesh
and became the God-Man. This didn't change or diminish
His deity, but it added to Him something He previously did
not have – a human body, with its attendant weaknesses.

[58] *Mickelson's Enhanced Strong's Dictionaries of the Greek and Hebrew Testaments.*
[59] Waldron, p. 57.
[60] Ibid, p. 59.

Hebrews 10 makes this clear, opening a review of why He had to come and put an end to sin, then this, in verse 5: *"Therefore, **as He was coming into the world**, He said: You did not want sacrifice and offering, but **You prepared a body for Me**."* As the Son was coming into the world, God the Father prepared a body for Him. When He was conceived in the virgin Mary, that is when Jesus was begotten – came to be a man. This agrees with Psalm 2 and Acts 13:33.

Waldron divides God into two parts: essence and personhood; claims they are different in scope and substance. He conflates this assertion with the hypostatic union, claiming both are at risk if we fail to agree with his position. Yet the biblical truth is the Son is eternally the Son and the Spirit eternally the Spirit just as the Father is eternally the Father. One eternal God, three eternal Persons. The son was begotten in the fullness of time, the Spirit was given (proceeded from) during Pentecost.

In chapter 7, on God's Covenant, Waldron argues at length for the "Covenant of Grace" without once examining its origin nor admitting the Bible has another term (the New Covenant). [61] Since the Bible gives us a term, and since "Covenant of Grace" has much theological baggage and needs much clarification – why use this term? One of his problems is the failure to see the dichotomous or dual nature of the Abrahamic Covenant. He claims the Abrahamic, Mosaic, and Davidic covenants are "organically related" to each other[62] and all must, therefore, have the same substance. These covenants are given to man by God – they are related in that, as is the New Covenant. While each of

---

[61] Waldron, p. 106-114.
[62] Ibid, p. 108-109.

these covenants have some things in common with the others, there are also differences.

The key is to see the Abrahamic Covenant as a coin (this is how John Bunyan described it), with the unconditional promise of Genesis 12 on one side and the conditional covenant of circumcision on the other side. The latter was swallowed up by the Mosaic Covenant. The promise is clearly seen in the New Testament as being fulfilled in the New Covenant, which entered history when Christ was crucified. Galatians 3:29 tells us that if we believe in Christ Jesus, we are Abraham's seed, heirs according to the promise. The Mosaic Covenant and the Davidic Covenant were works covenants. All the blessings were contingent on the human parties being faithful to their obligations. No mortal came out of these covenants having worked his way into God's favor. They were never intended for such. The Son of David who sits on the throne this day is the only One who came out of the Davidic Covenant with blessing in His hand.

To his credit, Waldron has not fallen into the Presbyterian rut of thinking infants are included in their covenant of grace. [63]

In chapter 10, Of Effectual Calling, Waldron defends the confession's statement in paragraph 3: "Elect infants dying in infancy are regenerated and saved by Christ through the Spirit; who works when, and where, and how He pleases; so also are all elect persons, who are incapable of being outwardly called by the ministry of the Word."[64] Yet, a bit further on, he says this: "The fact is that the Bible is silent on this issue. It would have been much better, therefore, for the confession simply to say nothing at this point. For that, I

---

[63] Waldron, p. 111.
[64] Ibid,

am convinced, is precisely what the Bible says."[65] I am grateful for his candor and honesty here; I think the paragraphs he wrote in defense of the language would have been better left unwritten and his simple observation of truth remain.

In chapter 17, on The Perseverance of the Saints, Waldron lists several "Tragic Fruits of Backsliding" with a stern warning: "Brethren, there is no guarantee that any one of us will not fall into such sins apart from perpetual watchfulness."[66] This is good counsel. The next sentence, not so good: "You may be a Christian, but that does not exclude the possibility that you may damn your children …"[67] It is clear to me that we ought to be careful what example and instruction we provide our children; it is beyond me how any who holds the doctrines of grace can think he can damn anyone. If man can damn one, he can save one. This is sloppy on Waldron's part, sloppy and very detrimental to parents who are not familiar with Scripture.

For chapter 19, a slight excursion to a short article I wrote while in elder training in a 1689 LBC congregation:

1689 LBC on the Law

(footnotes as they appear in Sam Waldron's *Modern Exposition*)

From chapter 19 of the Second London Baptist Confession.

Paragraph 1. God gave to Adam a law of universal obedience written in his heart. Agreed. The 1689 LBC refers to Genesis 1:27; Ecclesiastes 7:29; Romans 2:12a, 14-15 for this statement. The first two passages talk about man

---

[65] Waldron, p. 150.
[66] Ibid, p. 222.
[67] Ibid.

being made in God's image and upright; Romans reveals the law given to all men – Gentiles who were not given the Mosaic Covenant. This law given to Adam was given in conjunction with the Fall, for that is when man needed it. It is what I call God's universal law, what some call the law of nature or conscience.

Paragraph 2. The same law that was first written in the heart of man continued to be a perfect rule of righteousness after the fall. It was not written on man's heart until the Fall. Until sin entered, man was ruled by his unhindered relationship with YHWH – no need for a legal code. We see the universal law at work beginning in Genesis 3, continuing throughout biblical and world history. This law must be "the same law" referred to above, in Romans 2, because the confession says, "the same law". Yet the Scriptures referenced point to various places where the Mosaic Law is written in Scripture, not Adam's heart. The balance of this paragraph declares that the Ten Words given on Sinai are the same law as written on Adam's heart – citing the same passage from Romans which reveals the law at work in Gentiles who do not have the law of Moses.

How can the law given Adam be the law of the Gentiles, who are without the law of Moses, then be described as the Ten Words which were given to Moses as law that the Jews had possession of? And how does using Romans 2:12a & 14-15 as the proof text prove that? Other versions of the 1689 LBC refer to Deuteronomy 10 – which describes the tablets but does not indicate that they are the same law as given to Adam. This is conjecture, not exegesis. And it conflicts with itself regardless of which "proof texts" are used in a given version of the confession.

Paragraph 3. Besides this law, commonly called moral ... There is no proof text for this assertion, that the ten words are the moral law. It appears that the previous reference to the ten words given on Sinai is "this law" being here mentioned. What is the biblical defense for the Decalogue being called *the* moral law? Are there not ceremonial and/or civil law within it, varying to a small degree between the two records of the Decalogue? Where in Scripture is the Decalogue declared to be the law written in the heart of man? Rather than being "the moral law" of God, it would seem that the Decalogue is a particular application of the God's law to the Jews.

Paragraph 5. The moral law does for ever bind all, as well justified persons as others, to the obedience thereof. We cannot understand the meaning of this statement without knowing what was meant by the word, "bind". Which of these definitions (from a modern dictionary, but in alignment with Webster's 1828 dictionary) applies to the law of Moses and the Christian?

> *a* : to make secure by tying
> *b* : to confine, restrain, or restrict as if with bonds
> *c* : to put under an obligation <*binds* himself with an oath>
> *d* : to constrain with legal authority

I do not find anything in the Bible performing any of these functions of the law of Moses for the Christian, though the last definition certainly applies the Mosaic Law to all persons who were in the Mosaic Covenant.

The footnotes for this assertion mention a Jew trying to keep the law of Moses (Matt. 19:16-22); the same Romans passage as above – having to do with Gentiles without the law of Moses; Jews who are condemned by the law of Moses (Rom. 3:19-20); Christians who now *"serve in the new way of the Spirit and not in the old way of the written code."*

(Rom. 7:6) – what else could this "written code" be if not the law of Moses? Next is a verse attesting to the victory we have in God (Rom. 8:3); and Paul's statement that the law is good if used lawfully (1 Tim. 1:8-11) – is "using the law lawfully" the same as "binding all people" with it?

If Christians are freed from the condemnation of the law, and live in the new way of the Spirit, then lawful use of the law (and it does appear Paul means the law of Moses) is to be used to restrain and punish the lawless and disobedient, the ungodly and sinners, and myriad others who engage in gross sin. This does not say the law of Moses is used to bind all people to the obedience thereof – it is to bind those who are not in Christ or rebellious against God; those are the people this text tells us the law is for.

The next citation has Paul summing up the second table of the law of Moses as doing no wrong to a neighbor, which is proper love for one another (Rom. 13:8-10); then we see the law of Moses held up as the perfect standard of obedience (1 Cor. 7:19) – which is possible only for the Lord Jesus; and then we are referred to two statements in which circumcision (often a summary of the law of Moses) is described as nothing, but faith in Christ as the only thing that matters (Gal. 5:6 & 6:15). Then we have a large section of Ephesians (4:25 – 6:4) which does not mention the law of Moses but does show the demands of God's commands; and James 2:11-12 – which shows us the condemnation of the law of Moses contrasted with "the law of liberty" under which Christians shall be judged. Christians are not bound and judged by the law of Moses; we are informed by it. We are bound by and judged by the law of liberty, which only comes by being set free from the penalty of sin by being made a new creature in Christ – not having our sins charged against us.

This paragraph ends with, **neither does Christ in the Gospel in any way dissolve, but much strengthen this obligation**; meaning the obligation and binding of the Mosaic law is greater for the Christian. Matthew 5:17-19 is cited, which refers to the totality of the Old Covenant law which the Jewish leaders were to teach and live – it does not bind Christians to obedience to the law of Moses. Then we are led to Romans 3:31, where man's inability to keep the law of Moses and the prophets is said by Paul to establish the law – confirm it as God's covenant that must be kept by those to whom that covenant was made. The law – in total – stands as vindication of man's inability to justify himself, opposing the Jews and the Gentiles.

Paragraph 6 sums up a very defensible perspective on the law and the Christian (apart from the word, "bind"). It would be most useful if the term "the law" were defined. Assuming the Decalogue to be thus is something that warrants careful support from Scripture, not presupposition based on what the paedobaptists have written.

In summary, I believe the 1689 LBC suffers from paedobaptist influence in its perception of The Law, resulting in unavoidable conflicts within itself. Baptists ought not to embrace this unless we embrace their view of the covenants as well, for therein lies the basis for the view espoused in this chapter.

Back to a few more examples from Waldron's exposition. Waldron tells us that chapter 20, "Of the gospel and the extent of the grace therein … is the only entirely new chapter in the Baptist Confession not contained in any form in the Westminster Confession. This chapter does not, however, originate with the Baptists. It was the Congregational Puritans who wrote it and inserted in the Savoy Declaration in 1658."[68] Two things: first, this ought to stop the protest of those who keep insisting the 1689 LBC is not a clone of the Westminster; second, this also shows the truth of the introduction of the 1689 LBC, wherein the authors advertised their agreement with the WCF and the Savoy, having the same faith and doctrine with them.

In chapter 22, "Of religious worship and of the sabbath day," Waldron wrote, "The Confession teaches that the law of nature requires an appointed day for worship. Two things should be evident by the light of nature. First, God must be worshipped publicly and corporately by men. Second, such public and corporate worship requires a publicly and corporately agreed upon proportion of time. … the law of nature does not and cannot specify which day that should be. Resting for worship on the seventh day or first day is not written by creation on the hearts of men."[69]

I do not see anything in the Bible that reveals this law of nature that Waldron speaks of; that which "requires an appointed day for worship" yet is unable to specify that day. Waldron does not tell us how he reconciles his view in chapter 22 with what is written in the confession in chapter 19:

> Paragraph 2. The same law that was first written in the heart of man continued to be a perfect rule of righteousness after the fall, and was delivered by God upon Mount Sinai, in ten commandments, and written in two tables, the four first containing our duty towards God, and the other six, our duty to man.

If the tablets of stone were written on the heart of man prior to the fall, and it spells out the seventh day as the Sabbath,

---

[68] Waldron, p. 245.
[69] Ibid, p. 273.

how is it that, in speaking of the sabbath, Waldron tells us the day is not and cannot be specified? In this theological construct, the law of nature is not needed – the tablets of stone are set in our hearts. This is yet another point of tension in this system, which the second generation of Particular Baptists took from the Westminster folk. The Bible tells us that the Sabbath was given by God to the nation of Israel at Mt. Sinai (Nehemiah 9:13-14), not from the garden. How is it a creation ordinance if not given to man until Sinai? Further, in the second giving of the law, Moses declared that the law – including the Decalogue – was not given prior to Mt. Horeb/Sinai. *"Moses summoned all Israel and said to them, "Israel, listen to the statutes and ordinances I am proclaiming as you hear them today. Learn and follow them carefully. **The LORD our God made a covenant with us at Horeb. He did not make this covenant with our fathers, but with all of us who are alive here today.**"* (Deuteronomy 5:1-3, emphasis mine) The stone tablets, upon which were engraved the Decalogue, are described as *"**the words of the covenant**, ... tablets of the testimony."* (Exodus 34:28-29)

Two more observations about the "Christian Sabbath" found in the 1689 LBC. First, it's a sign; second, a sacrifice is needed.

1. A Sign. Some background to establish the importance of a sign. In Genesis 9:12-17, YHWH sets His rainbow in the sky as a sign of the covenant with all creation.

    *And God said, "**This is the sign of the covenant** I am making between Me and you and every living creature with you, **a covenant** for all future generations: I have placed **My bow in the clouds**, and it will be a **sign of the covenant** between Me and the earth. Whenever I form clouds over the earth and **the bow appears in the*** *clouds, I will remember **My covenant** between Me and you and all the living creatures: water will never again become a flood to destroy every creature. **The bow will be in the clouds**, and I will look at it and remember **the everlasting covenant** between God and all the living creatures on earth." God said to Noah, **"This is the sign of the covenant** that I have confirmed between Me and every creature on earth."*

Every Christian I know is adamant that the rainbow cannot be claimed by the radical homosexuals as a standard because God created the rainbow to serve as the sign of His covenant with creation. What God has spoken cannot be ripped out of Scripture and repurposed as man sees fit. Why, then, do Magisterial Reformers think it's OK to take the sign of Mosaic Covenant and repurpose it as they see fit? Ezekiel 20:10-12 *"So **I brought them out of the land of Egypt** and led them into the wilderness. Then I gave them My statutes and explained My ordinances to them — the person who does them will live by them. I also **gave them My Sabbaths to serve as a sign** between Me and them, so they will know that I am Yahweh who sets them apart as holy."* The system of Sabbath days was created by God to be a sign between Him and national Israel. Man cannot repurpose that sign any more than he can the rainbow.

2. The Sacrifice. Inherent in the weakly[70] Sabbaths given to Israel was the need for the priests to offer sacrifices. Numbers 28:9-10 *"**On the Sabbath day** [present] two unblemished year-old male lambs, four quarts of fine flour mixed with oil as a grain offering, and its drink*

---

[70] I use this spelling to convey the idea that the Law commanded rest but is unable to provide rest; it's weak.

61

*offering. It is the burnt offering for **every Sabbath**, in addition to the regular burnt offering and its drink offering.*" I know of no Reformers who grapple with this Sabbath requirement.

The near complete disconnect between the Reformed confessions teaching on the weekly Sabbath and the biblical description and requirements for that day is profound. These documents claim the continuing practice of the weekly Sabbath but have introduced a faux-Sabbath built not on Scripture, but upon man's imagination. This is systematic theology run amuck.

We must stand with what is written in Scripture, not what our system of theology says.

Waldron goes on, in speaking of how the sabbath is commanded "one day in seven"[71] while the Bible records it specifically as THE seventh day: "*the **seventh day** is a Sabbath to the LORD your God.*" (Exodus 20:10) Christian sabbatarians play games with what the Bible says because they have moved the weakly sabbath from Saturday (the seventh day) to Sunday (the first day). Further, they have redefined what conduct the "Christian Sabbath" requires – see **Appendix 2 – A Tale of Two Sabbaths** for a comparison of these. If you think the rest we come to when the Spirit brings us to Christ is a day of the week, you are grasping at shadows rather than resting in the Lord of the Sabbath; He is the substance the weakly Sabbath pointed to.

Waldron also tells us: "The Ten Commandments have an importance that transcends the Old Testament laws (see chapter 19). They alone were directly spoken by God."[72]. This assertion is blatantly false! One example overthrows

---

[71] Waldron, p. 273.
[72] Ibid.

this false statement: "*God blessed Noah and his sons and said to them, "Be fruitful and multiply and fill the earth."* (Genesis 9:1) This is the same construction as the "covenant of works" wherein we read, "*God blessed them, and God said to them, "Be fruitful, multiply, fill the earth."* (Genesis 1:28). When God commands man to do something, it is the same concept as "law" which is one of several ways to interpret "torah." The primary meaning of Torah is "a teaching precept or statute." God spoke many times to many people, giving them "teaching precepts" or "statutes" or "laws." Laws given in covenant context are bound to that covenant. Covenant laws do not have force of law outside their covenants; they may certainly serve as revelation to us, even though they are not law for us. See **Appendix 3 - The Decalogue Contrasted with The Law of Christ** for how Scripture bears this out.

We further read from Waldron's pen, "It is now evident why the Lord's day must be viewed as the Christian sabbath. The institution of the sabbath at creation, the inclusion of the sabbath in the Decalogue and the continuation of the sabbath principle in the Lord's day demand this. ... we must distinguish between the Jewish seventh-day sabbath ordinance, which is abolished, and the concept of the sabbath, which is continued on the Lord's day."[73] Not all Magisterial Reformers agreed with the idea of a creation ordinance sabbath; John Calvin made no mention of it in his *Institutes*. It appears Calvin was unsure about the observance of the Sabbath by the ancient patriarchs. "It is questionable," he writes, "whether it had already been observed by the patriarchs."[74] Deuteronomy 5:1.5 declares that God did not make the covenant, of which the Sabbath was a sign, with

---

[73] Waldron, p. 275.
[74] John Calvin, *Moses*, 2:271.

the fathers and, in Nehemiah 9:13-14, we read: *You came down on Mount Sinai, and spoke to them from heaven. You gave them* impartial ordinances, reliable instructions, and good statutes and commands. *You revealed Your holy Sabbath to them, and gave them commands,* statutes, and instruction *through Your servant Moses.* Nowhere do we read that the covenant or its sign was given to anyone other than national Israel.

God rested on the 7th day (not one day in seven) and used that as an example of why the nation of Israel was to rest on the 7th day – not "one day in seven."

Note this: nowhere in Scripture is any day called the "Christian sabbath." To lean on the one occurrence of *"the Lord's Day"* (Revelation 1:10) as the foundation for claiming the first day of the week as the "Christian sabbath" is without exegetical reasoning. This is what "full subscription" to a confession looks like. Further, it is clear from Scripture that we are a holy people, set aside by God for His service; not a cultic people bound to holy places or holy days, which are marks of pagan religions. See **Appendix 5 – Holy People**, for an examination of this topic.

The blind bias against any connection with Anabaptists in any form shows up in Waldron's comments in chapter 24, "Of the civil magistrate," where he said, "Our Baptist forefathers were not Anabaptists."[75] He bases this on the Anabaptist view that Christians are not to serve in government office. He ignores the common ground with some Anabaptists, which history shows interaction on, regarding believers' baptism, local autonomy, and liberty of conscience.[76] History is not so orderly that one can credibly

---

[75] Waldron, p. 288.
[76] See Appendix 1 – The Anabaptist Connection.

exclude a group of people from their heritage when there was much interaction. The desire to do so reveals a confidence in the flesh, as if proving a fleshly connection with the preferred people enhances one's own standing. This reminds me of the sandy foundation of the Jews in Jesus' day, who bragged about being fleshly children of Abraham.

This bias shows up again in chapter 26, "Of the church," where Waldron talks about sharing this doctrine with the Savoy Congregationalists, "The ideas found in this chapter are, then, not exclusively those of Baptists, but ideas advocated by such Congregationalist Puritans as Thomas Goodwin, John Owen, John Cotton and Jonathan Edwards."[77] He completely ignores the shared view with most Anabaptists on this matter. Waldron's consistent bias is to embrace the baby-sprinklers as the theological fathers of his faith, ignoring the long-standing doctrines of some Anabaptists which align very well with what Particular Baptists believe. I've read comments from several Magisterial Reformers who state not many Anabaptists were in England during these developmental times. Historical accounts do not line up with this view:

> By 1535, there were many Dutch Anabaptists living in England, and thereafter their numbers increased steadily. The proportion who were Anabaptists is unknown, but in 1562 Dutch people in England numbered 30,000.[78] Gregory records that between 50,000 and 100,000 Dutch refugees came to England in the period of the struggle of the Netherlands against Alva.[79] They came in largest numbers when persecution was greatest in their country and when

---

[77] Waldron, p. 311.
[78] Walker, *Creeds and Platforms of Congregationalism*, 6.
[79] *Puritanism in the Old World and the New*, 204.

England offered the most promising refuge, and they congregated in East Coast centers such as London, Norwich (where they were a majority of the population in 1587),[80] Dover, Romeney. Sandwich, Canterbury, Colchester, and Hastings. Not all were found to be in the East, for many went to work in the wooden industry in the West.[81] Few of these immigrants ever repatriated themselves; most of them were assimilated by the English, losing their identity.[82]

This brief account does not prove Anabaptist influence on either Baptist confession, but it does show that there were enough Anabaptists in country and London to make it very feasible. To ignore it or sweep it aside without examination simply proves bias.

I set out two reasons for this review: First, with many words comes increased opportunity for error. Second, many 1689 advocates assert a theological heritage narrowly aligned with the Puritans, declaiming any connection to those called Anabaptist. Again, my aim is not to ridicule Mr. Waldron or the 1689 LBC; it is to show this document is not wholly biblical or Baptist nor wholly accurate in its assumptions about history.

Back to Samuel Renihan's book for a look at how he sees the doctrine of the 1689 LBC.

His introduction to Chapter Two brings to light another example of why I find academic books so tedious. Renihan uses foreign language terms he is familiar with, as if all who might read his book are also familiar with them. In many

---

[80] Walker, *supra*.
[81] Whitley, *Minutes of the General Assembly of Ge. Bapts.*, xl.
[82] Lumpkin, p. 13.

cases, he puts these words in italics to show they are not standard English fare – such as *foedus legale*, which he explains means "legal covenant." In this introduction, he uses "credenda" without giving us any hint as to what it means – not even putting it in italics to notify us it isn't English. "Credenda" rhymes with "agenda" – this appears to be the reason he used it; he did not choose it to communicate meaning to the reader. "Credenda" is a Latin word that means "a system of beliefs." "Doctrine" is a handy term for that idea, but it doesn't rhyme with agenda. Rant over.

It is so important for Renihan to reinforce his pristine idea that these first-generation particular Baptists were "Puritans" that he attributes to them a "Puritan zeal" in their pursuit of biblical truth. Like many Anabaptists, these early Particular Baptists agreed with much, but not all, of Baptist doctrines the Magisterial Reformers wrote. I have not found one first-generation particular Baptist who described his position as "Puritan," as if identifying with those people was important to his own identity.

Ritor pointed to the unique nature of Abraham's role, highlighting that he was a pattern of belief to all future believers, and privileged to be the father of the nation that would produce the promised seed, Jesus Christ, through whom the nations would be blessed. Given these factors, the covenant was not made with him upon belief, though it highlighted his faith, nor was circumcision administered to him and his seed when he became a believer. In fact, Ritor argued, the covenant had already been established with Abraham in Genesis 12 more than twenty years before the institution of circumcision. It was illegitimate to make "believers and their children" a pattern of covenant polity based on Abraham's example. Ritor stated,

And therefore although the Covenant and Promises were made to Abraham, and his seed, yet the consequence will not follow, that the Covenant is likewise made with all Beleevers and their seed, for Beleevers only are the seed, and the seed only, and none of them a Father in the Gospell sence, nor any other, save only Abraham to whom and his seed the Covenant and Promises are made.[83]

"The analogy that Ritor is setting up is a twofold view of the Abrahamic covenant. On the one hand, promises were made to Abraham as an earthly father and his seed. On the other hand, promises were made to Abraham as a paradigmatic believer and his seed, i.e., those who believe as he did. Confusing the seeds of Abraham (Israelites and believers) was precisely the problem Ritor was addressing."[84]

In conclusion, Ritor's covenant theology should be viewed as a development within a larger English Puritan Protestant context. It stands in continuity with Reformed thought on the dogmatic contrast between the law and the gospel, connecting this to the old and new covenants. The most distinctive feature of his covenant theology was to deny that the covenant of circumcision is the covenant of grace through nuanced typology. This view will continue to mark out and distinguish the Particular Baptists from the paedobaptists.[85]

Blackwood took a step forward at this point. He argued that in Genesis 17 "the new Covenant is promised but not covenanted, which promise before

---

[83] Ritor, *The Second Part of the Vanity*, 18.
[84] Samuel Renihan, p. 60.
[85] Ibid, p. 63.

was made to Adam, Noah, Abraham."[86] Citing
Jeremiah 31 he continued, "He saith not, I have made
a covenant, but I will make a new Covenant which
was made good at the death of Christ, as the Apostle
makes it appear, Heb. 8:9, 10 repeating this place of
Jeremiah."[87] That the covenant of grace, or new
covenant, existed only in the form of a promise had
not been asserted previously by Particular Baptists.
Ritor had spoken of two covenants in Genesis 17,
distinguished by their spiritual and earthly promises.
Spilsbury had distinguished the promises, but not
into two covenants. Blackwood clearly distinguished
the covenants, but likewise distinguished the new
Covenant into a pre-messianic promise form, and a
post-messianic established covenantal form[88].

I am more in agreement with Blackwood on this point than I
am with Spilsbury. I see the covenant with Abraham as two-
sided, as did John Bunyon. The unconditional promise being
fulfilled in the New Covenant, upon the death and
resurrection of Jesus Christ; the conditional covenant of
circumcision being swallowed up by the Mosaic Covenant.

In the Introduction of the Chapter Three, Renihan gives an
overview of the civil war that plagued England in the early
to mid-17th century[89]. He does not mention Oliver Cromwell
and the Fifth Monarchy movement which drew men in from
every religious stripe, including particular Baptists. I will not
ask you to read multiple pages reviewing Renihan's bias in

---

[86] Blackwood, *The Storming of Antichrist*, 68. Later he said, "If this
Covenant with Abram was the Covenant of grace, yet was it made with
the children of promise onely, which are believers of Jew and Gentile,
and not their seed."
[87] Samuel Renihan, p. 35.
[88] Ibid, p. 73.
[89] Ibid, p. 82.

ignoring Anabaptist and General Baptist influence on the authors of the 1644 LBC; the reality of this is documented in several ways and places in this book.

When Renihan gets to examining the authors of the 2nd LBC, he does mention a General Baptist (Henry Danvers)[90] and acknowledges that he had an impact on a Particular Baptist (Edward Hutchinson),[91] although we are not told what impact that was. Renihan covers many pages exploring the conflict between these second-generation Particular Baptists and their paedobaptist counterparts – particularly on the topic of water baptism. It is quite a good read.

Renihan documents the fact that the 2nd LBC was drafted up in August, 1677. He says:

> This confession followed, word for word in most chapters, the Westminster Confession and the Savoy Declaration. The Particular Baptists did this "the more abundantly, to manifest our consent with both, in all the fundamental articles of the Christian Religion."[92]

It seems this second generation of Particular Baptists saw fit to distance themselves from Thomas Collier, after he departed from orthodox Christianity. State-church folk enjoying smearing them with Collier's heresy, much as they did the earlier Particular Baptists with "Anabaptist" leanings.

Renihan further comments on this August, 1677 meeting:

---

[90] Samuel Renihan, p. 115.
[91] Ibid, p. 116.
[92] Ibid, p. 137. The quote within Renihan's statement is from the 2nd LBC, *iv of an unpaginated preface.*

This historical context is important for appreciating the Baptists' choices in the covenant theology of their second Confession of Faith. It was not a polemical document seeking to distance the Baptists from Presbyterians and Independents, but a declaration of agreement in the fundamental articles of the Christian religion. The covenant theology of 2LCF, much like 1LCF, revolved primarily around the core doctrines of Protestant covenant theology and avoided, for the most part, the distinctive opinions of the Particular Baptists.[93]

If the totality of the 2nd LBC is within "the fundamental articles of the Christian religion," and the "Protestant covenant theology" contained therein is part and parcel of those "fundamental articles of the faith," then why was this system of covenants not known to man prior to the 16th century, when Ulrich Zwingli developed the confusing "Covenant of Grace" to convince himself of infant baptism, so-called?[94] In associating their system with that of the Westminster and Savoy congregations, and avoiding "the distinctive opinions of the Particular Baptists," Renihan appears to think the Presbyterian system is superior to that documented by Baptists. This is my impression, being trained in a 1689 LBC congregation for service as an elder. This is why I cannot embrace the 1689 LBC.

Renihan dismisses Baptist disagreement on the mythical "Covenant of Works" made with Adam before the fall (see discussion earlier in this chapter), claiming any mention of covenant with Adam is the same as this Presbyterian "Covenant of Works," by which Adam could have earned

---

[93] Samuel Renihan, p. 138.
[94] See this author's book, *In Darkness – Light!*, pages 142-145 for details. https://www.amazon.com/dp/0998655961

eternal life. Agreeing to Adam's federal headship of mankind is not the same thing as agreeing to the "Covenant of Works." Renihan: "In some writings, the term itself is not used but Adam is called a "publick person," and understood to stand in a role of federal headship over mankind. The human race received Adam's guilt and his fallen nature."[95]

He doesn't admit that the 2nd LBC mentions the "Covenant of Works" without defining it; he claims the 2nd LBC doesn't shy "away from the covenant of works, but a clearer confession of it." A clearer confession of a covenant without defining it. The fact that this confession rightly sees God as having "absolute dominion over his creation," is heralded as if that proves a "Covenant of Works." You will search the Scripture in vain, looking for this "reward" offered to Adam, but "they confessed, God did "by way of covenant." Having confessed in chapter 6 that Adam's obedience to the law would have been "unto life," in chapter 7 the Particular Baptists confessed that this work-reward relationship was possible only through a covenant."[96] So a promise not found in Scripture is valid because a covenant not found in Scripture says so. This is not how one exegetes the Scripture.

Renihan goes on to discuss the other mythical covenant found in the Presbyterian system, the "Covenant of Grace." "There was no doctrinal difference between the Particular Baptists and the Westminster and Savoy divines regarding the covenant of works. Likewise, from a dogmatic standpoint, there was no disagreement between them regarding the covenant of works' counterpart, the covenant of grace."[97] Cognitive dissonance is strong with this author, for on the next page Renihan says, "The Particular Baptists

---

[95] Samuel Renihan, p. 139.
[96] Ibid, p. 141.
[97] Ibid, p. 142.

often used this underlying dogmatic unity to argue against any model of the covenant of grace that included the non-elect or permitted its members to fall away from the covenant. By confessing the exact same doctrine of the covenant of grace, dogmatically, the Particular Baptists intentionally placed themselves within Reformed covenantalism. But their paths parted when speaking historically of the covenant of grace."[98] Further, he says, "The key difference between these confessions is the Particular Baptists' complete avoidance of distinguishing the covenant of grace into two historical administrations. In their "quill-skirmishes," the Particular Baptists had repeatedly rejected the idea that the old covenant was the covenant of grace in a different form."[99] He had just claimed "there was no disagreement between them regarding the covenant of works' counterpart, the covenant of grace." He said these later Baptists confessed "the exact same doctrine of the covenant of grace." And then he details the DIFFERENCES they have with the Presbyterian "covenant of grace." One cannot claim both of these at the same time.

Renihan later reports, "In their Confession, the Particular Baptists directly tied the covenant of grace to the gospel. Where the gospel is found, there is the covenant of grace. As the gospel was progressively made known throughout history, the covenant of grace was progressively made known throughout history."[100] Here's a suggestion, use biblical terms when appropriate. The way the 1689 LBC describes the "covenant of grace" shows they have a different covenant than the Presbyterians do – it is NOT "the exact same doctrine." There is a LACK of complete agreement. The Bible calls out the New Covenant where the

---

[98] Samuel Renihan, p. 143.
[99] Ibid, p. 144.
[100] Ibid.

1689 LBC calls out a "covenant of grace." Yes, the New Covenant is a grace covenant – but it's never called by the name, Covenant of Grace. By using this label, the 1689 LBC authors set themselves up for a never-ending argument in which they have to explain why their "covenant of grace" is not the same one the Presbyterians made up.

I will bring this to a close with one more example from Renihan. In describing the period in which the confession was being drafted, Renihan:

> It was a time requiring unification, restoration, and public vindication. This they accomplished in their Confession of Faith in which they expressed agreement with Reformed orthodoxy regarding the covenants of works and grace. They avoided the language of substance and administration but offered a broad covenantal model in its place. The confusion of recent writers and the broadness of the confession left a need for a careful expression of Particular Baptist covenant theology, one that would clear the confusion and take the Particular Baptists into the next generation. Nehemiah Coxe supplied that need. To understand Nehemiah Coxe's covenant theology, however, it is necessary to understand the developments of covenant theology in his day. In particular, it is necessary to examine the foundation upon which he built, John Owen's covenant theology."[101]

These Baptists rightly refused to go along with the paedobaptists' "language of substance and administration" but they ran right back to the paedobaptists to more fully develop their "Baptist" view of covenants. This was the

---

[101] Samuel Renihan, p. 148.

pattern for this second generation of Particular Baptists. Borrow as much as you can from the paedobaptists and argue over shared terms and authors.

Another brother, from a different camp of Particular Baptists, made this helpful observation:

> In closing, I think it is significant to observe what happened in John Murray's booklet, The Covenant of Grace. His biblical-theological study led him to see in Scripture a plurality of covenants (p.26) culminating in the finality of the New Covenant (pp.28,31-32). He nowhere found in the Bible "one covenant of grace" variously administered. To be sure, in his other writings he states that such a covenant exists. But he did not find it in his Scriptural study with the title The Covenant of Grace. He uses only the phrase "covenant grace," but never "the covenant of grace." This again suggests the propriety of seeing "covenants" as historical manifestations, and of avoiding a "covenant of grace" which stands above history. If we stick with the Biblical presentation of one "purpose" in Christ, and a plurality of covenants in history, we will avoid the confusion of Dispensationalism's earthly-purpose-for-Israel, heavenly-purpose-for-church theory, and the unnecessary assumptions of Covenant Theology which are used to bring infants into the New Covenant church.[102]

When advocates of a doctrine have trouble being consistent in how that doctrine works out in Scripture, that's when you know there's a faulty foundation under that doctrine. When a majority of doctrine is copied from the paedobaptist

---

[102] Jon Zens, "Is There a Covenant of Grace?", Conclusion.

world, there will be much conjecture and inference. Building on conjecture and inference results in a shaky doctrine. This is not the Baptist way; do not walk in it.

5. Comparison of the Two Confessions

When our children were young, there was a song on the TV show Sesame Street that went along with a teaching on how to discern differences among things were somewhat alike. The song's refrain was "One of these things is not like the other". That sums up this chapter!

One of these things is NOT like the others!

The preface to the 1689 LBC confirms that it is patterned after and is in large agreement with the WCF and SD. I have documented how 81% of the content of the 1689 LBC came from those two documents and about 4% came from the 1644 LBC. One of these things is NOT LIKE the others!

45 of the 53 articles of the 1644 LBC correlate to paragraphs in the 1689 LBC, even though there is not specific phrasing in common. The topics and – largely – the positions taken may provide a valid foundation for saying these two Baptist confessions are "substantially in agreement" as is claimed by the 1689 LBC as the 2nd agrees with most of the 1st.

At the same time, the differences in these shared articles shows substantial lack of agreement. One example, mentioned earlier: The 1644 LBC is much more focused on the multi-faceted roles of Christ Jesus: prophet, priest, king, and mediator; the 1689 LBC focuses on Him as mediator.

Additionally, the 1689 LBC has 18 complete chapters and 114 paragraphs that have no correlation to the 1644 LCB. These are topics the 1644 LBC simply does not address and, therefore, cannot represent agreement or disagreement. Marriage and the Lord's Supper are examples, as are Mosaic Law and the Covenant of Works. One cannot assert agreement on topics that are missing from one document.

Many advocates of the 1689 LBC claim that it and the 1st LBC are "substantially the same". James Renihan makes this statement:

> It is troubling to read statements asserting or inferring that there is some form of theological difference between these two great confessions. Some seem to think that the 1644/46 Confession is more authentically Baptist, while the Second Confession is less so. Most often, this is asserted by those who dislike the Covenant theology that is more explicit in the Second Confession than in the First. It is especially true of those who espouse the so-called "New Covenant" theology.[103]

Renihan would be "troubled" by this chapter. He described editing procedures that he claims were common to these two confessions as proof that the content is the same. Common editing procedures does not equate to common content. He also conflates the 1644 LBC with the 1646 revision, as this gives him more common authors to undergird his assertion. He uses father-son relationships to imagine identical

---

[103] James Renihan, "No Substantial Theological Difference between the First and Second London Baptist Confessions."

theological views were maintained. Also, he thinks the buildings used in the 1640s, being used by different congregations in the 1660s and 1670s, carries unchanged theology and doctrine.

> Seven London congregations published the 1644/46 Confession. By 1689, representatives of 4 of these churches also publicly signed the 1689 Confession. What happened to the other 3? They either ceased to exist, or had merged into the remaining churches. In addition, several key men signed both Confessions: William Kiffin, Hanserd Knollys, and Henry Forty, as well as the father-son duo of Benjamin and Nehemiah Coxe. If the theology of the two Confessions is different, one would have to demonstrate that these churches and these men went through a process of theological change. **But no evidence for such exists.**[104] (emphasis mine)

Of the signatories of both confessions listed by Renihan, only Kiffin signed the 1644 LBC. The implication that congregations do not change over time is ludicrous. I serve in a congregation that has undergone significant change in the last 20 years, moving away from the "Christian Sabbath" and tithing. I've been in several congregations that have changed doctrines over the years. I know of several fathers and sons with significantly different views on doctrines. This is normal life. Renihan imagines ab-normal life and claims it as foundation for his argument. He asserts no evidence of theological change exists, yet one man who he heralds as a signatory of the 2nd LBC did not see the 1st day of the week in the way the 1689 LBC describes it; this is documented in the life of William Kiffin, below. This is one scrap of

---

[104] James Renihan, "No Substantial Theological Difference between the First and Second London Baptist Confessions."

evidence Renihan says does not exists, simply because he did not see it. It was easy for me to find it. What Renihan does not do is compare the two confessions to see what they have in common. That is the acid-test. Chapter 3 provides an overview of this. Of the 15 men who signed the 1644 LBC, only William Kiffin was also a signatory to the 1689 LBC – a tenuous argument for theological equality between those two documents.

In his sermon from Proverbs 28:1, Paul Hobson (a signatory of the 1644 LBC) wrote, "That Souls made righteous by God are in the enjoyment of God transcendently bold."[105] In discussing the boldness mentioned in this proverb, Hobson observes several types of boldness that are not that which Scripture intends. One of these is "Legal boldness, attaining to such a degree of obedience to the Law, that I thought my self all most blameless, and herein I grew bold indeed, and I thought it was true boldness: but it was discovered this was not the true boldness neither."[106] This is typical of the view of the men who signed the 1644 LBC – a refutation of the idea that law-keeping was the rule of life for Christians. Rather, he says, "Whether saints are bound to duty; they by that very act of enjoying God, make themselves over to God, to be acted, and ruled by God: their own will ceases, and God's will is become one with theirs, and theirs with his; you cannot choose but love & act for God, for you are with God, in God."[107] Hobson held to a love relationship with God, not a law-based relationship.

In another place, Hobson clarifies his position:

---

[105] Paul Hobson, *Practical Divinity*, p. 10.
[106] Ibid, p. 13.
[107] Ibid, p. 17-18.

if you would be holy, throw your selves into the loves of God; this very enjoyment will give you an enlarged, a free, and broken heart; then sin will be hated from a new nature. God does not say "I love you, if you be holy"; but, "I love you to make you holy". Beloved, this is the new covenant that the Gospel holds out to us; and herein lies the power of the Gospel, to make of unrighteous, righteous, to work by love, not by constraint.

Men that never had experience of this life, they lay Laws, and Constraints upon men to duty, and know not the power of love.[108]

This reflects what the 1644 LBC says about how one comes to Christ, in Article 15:

That the tenders of the Gospel to the conversion of sinners,[(1)] is absolutely free, no way requiring, as absolutely necessary, any qualifications, preparations, terrors of the Law, or preceding ministry of the Law, but only and alone the naked soul, as a[(2)] sinner and ungodly to receive Christ, as Christ, as crucified, dead, and buried, and risen again, being made[(3)] a Prince and a Savior for such sinners.

1) John 3:14, 15; 1:12; Isa. 55:1; John 7:37
2) 1 Tim. 1:15; Rom. 4:5; 5:8
3) Acts 5:30-31; 2:36; 1 Cor. 1:22-24

More from Paul Hobson, showing a view of law different from the 1689 LBC:

---

[108] Paul Hobson, *Practical Divinity*, p. 20.

That Religion which is in reference to a Law without, and not answering to a Law and a power of love within, is as when men have not only the light of reason, but convictions from the light of a Law, which sets men at work, not rightly understanding this Law without, from the power and spirit of a Law within. ... This is such a religion that men who live in it, may fall from it. But those saints who act in religious acts suitable to Christ, the Law being written in them, which is a rule for them; and the Law that regulates them is an act, is the Spirit, and Life and Power of the act; and so Christ is all in all.[109]

A law-based religion is without spiritual life.

When Renihan quoted William Kiffin, he selectively cited Kiffin's commentary on Hosea without providing any context:

in Scripture men are said to forsake God when they forsake the Law of God, the Commandments of God, or the worship of God . . . (page 4), to keep close to God is to keep close to the Law of God, the Commandments of God . . . it is best both with persons & churches, when they do so (page 16).[110]

The first citation is clearly speaking about people in the Mosaic Covenant community, not Christians, as Kiffin reveals. Right after Renihan's first citation, we read from Kiffin, "and therefore saith the Lord to Moses, this people will rise up, and go a whoring after the gods of a strange land, and will forsake me and break my covenant which I have made with them."[111] These were not Christians, but

---

[109] Paul Hobson, Letter – Spirit Distinctions.
[110] James Renihan, "No Substantial Theological Difference between the First and Second London Baptist Confessions."
[111] William Kiffin, *Certain Observations upon Hosea the Second.*

rebellious Jews! The second citation by Renihan is Kiffin using Hosea 2:7 as a model for how we are to return to God – "it will be better for us". What is not explicit in Kiffin's commentary is his meaning for the phrases, "Law of God" and "Commandments of God." It is presumptuous to claim to know for certain that Kiffin was expressing agreement with the WCF/1689 LBC view of covenants and law. Thomas Patient, another signer of the 1644 LBC, shows us a use of those terms, relating them to laws and commands in the New Testament, not the law of Moses (see below).

Some insight on Kiffin, from his own pen. William Kiffin reviewed his service with a congregation in Towerhill; when the meeting was disturbed. "I was generally kept out of the hands of the persecutors. But meeting one ***Lord's day*** at a house on Towerhill, on coming out, several rude persons were about the door; and many stones were flung at me which did me no hurt-only one fell upon my eye, but without any great prejudice; so I escaped out of their hands."[112] (emphasis mine) A few lines later, Kiffin described his time in the White Lyon prison, when some fellow prisoners sought to take his life. "Accordingly, on a ***Lord's-day***, in the evening, several of them came up to my chamber, my door being open, and only myself, my wife, a maid servant and child in the room. One Jackson, a noted rogue, came before them, having a great truncheon in his hand."[113] (emphasis mine) What I find remarkable is that Kiffin used the term "Lord's day" and not "sabbath." If, as James Renihan asserts, William Kiffin had the 1689 LBC view of law, he would have called those days "sabbath" or "Christian Sabbath," for that is the 1689 LBC terminology. Perhaps Kiffin's view of that day changed later in his life; perhaps not.

---

[112] William Kiffin, *Remarkable Passages in the Life of William Kiffin*, chapter II.
[113] Ibid.

John Spilsbury is another 1644 LBC signatory that James Renihan claims supports his view. Is this accurate? In the editor's introduction to Spilsbury's treatise on baptism, we read: "John Spilsbury distinguished rightly between the First and Second Covenants. He showed that there were indeed two covenants rather than two administrations of one covenant. ... By a proper understanding of the covenants and their distinctness some of the following doctrines will be cleared up: law or grace, which is the rule of life for the believer."[114] In the first chapter of his treatise, Spilsbury wrote, under the heading of Basic Truths:

> As the Scriptures being a perfect rule of all things, both for faith and order; this I confess is a truth;
> And for the just and true consequences of Scripture, I do not deny;
> And the Covenant of life lying between God and Christ for all His Elect, I do not oppose.
> And that the outward profession of the said Covenant, had differed under several Periods, I shall not deny;
> And of the Scriptures speaking of the disannulling and abolishing the old Covenant, and making a new, is to be understood of the Period from Moses to Christ, and not of that from Abraham to Moses.[115]

James Renihan cites all but the last sentence of this citation and claims this shows Spilsbury and others "were committed to the same kind of Covenant Theology that is more explicitly articulated in the Second London Confession."[116]

---

[114] John Spilsbury, *A Treatise Concerning the Lawful Subject of Baptisme*, p. 2.
[115] Ibid, p. 18.
[116] James Renihan, "No Substantial Theological Difference between the First and Second London Baptist Confessions."

This treatise by Spilsbury is not on covenants, per se; it covers them as a means to expound water baptism. It is not possible to claim the brief citation as a certain agreement on the WCF/1689 LBC view on covenants. What Spilsbury meant by the fourth statement is not found in Spilsbury's document. It is presumptuous to claim that knowledge without providing a source for it.

Another signer of the 1644 LBC was Thomas Patient, who is said to have developed his view on covenants from John Spilsbury. In a work similar in concept to Spilsbury treatise, Patient wrote:

> My **first** ground is infant's baptism does **oppose itself** to the *express Laws*, and *Commands of the New Testament*. Whatsoever consequence **men** do draw from Scripture that **crosses the plain Commands of God** (to be sure) *cannot be of God*, but *such consequence must be (according to Scripture light) of Satan*, or at the best, from the *vision of a man's own heart.*"[117] (emphasis original)

It's clear from this quote that Patient saw "laws and commands of the New Testament" the same as "Commands of God;" he was not referring to Old Covenant law. We cannot be dogmatic and claim that all the signers of the 1644 LBC had this same view; but we can say this is evidence that some of them had different views of law and covenants than is found in the 1689 LBC. And it's clear that the 1644 LBC does not teach on law and covenants as does the 1689 LBC. We are left without confirmation that they are "substantially the same".

As pointed out in chapter 1, the Magisterial Reformers do not agree with the 1644 LBC view of Mosaic Law. Two

---

[117] Thomas Patient, *The Doctrine of Baptism and the Distinction of the Covenants*, p. 24.

things account for this difference: 1.) The Magisterial Reformers clung to Thomas Aquinas' invention of a tripartite Mosaic Law. 2.) The King James Bible's translation of Galatians 3:24.

Firstly, the tripartite view of Mosaic Law facilitates a misapplication of that law, wherein the Tablets of Stone are called "Moral Law" and applied to all men. This use of the Tablets of the Covenant is not revealed in Scripture and the application of them by the 1689 LBC leaves the God-given punishments for violation of these commands behind. Men put themselves in the place of God, installing different punishments than He prescribed – because they try in vain to impose Old Covenant law as law upon those in the New Covenant. The truth is, we are informed by all of Scripture and see clearly in myriad places therein that God has forbidden and hates murder, theft, adultery, etc. The Old Covenant was based on fear of conviction for law-breaking, *to darkness, gloom, and storm, to the blast of a trumpet, and the sound of words. (Those who heard it begged that not another word be spoken to them, for they could not bear what was commanded: And if even an animal touches the mountain, it must be stoned!* (Hebrews 12:18b-20). The New Covenant has a higher calling, based on better promises; we *have come to Mount Zion, to the city of the living God (the heavenly Jerusalem), to myriads of angels in festive gathering, to the assembly of the firstborn whose names have been written in heaven, to God who is the Judge of all, to the spirits of righteous people made perfect, to Jesus (mediator of a new covenant), and to the sprinkled blood, which says better things than the blood of Abel.* (Hebrews 12:22-24).

The biblical stance on law is simple: The law written on stone tablets was given to people with stone hearts who worshiped God in a stone temple; this is the Old Covenant. In the New Covenant, a new law is written on tablets of flesh on the new hearts given to a spiritual people who are the eternal temple of God. This is the reality of what we read in Ezekiel 36:26 and in Hebrews 7:11-12: *If then, perfection came through the Levitical priesthood (for under it the people received the law), what further need was there for another priest to appear, said to be in the order of Melchizedek and not in the order of Aaron? For when there is a change of the priesthood, there must be a change of law as well.* The New Covenant was established by a new priesthood; this required a new law, reflecting the two greatest commands as seen through the life and teaching of our Great High Priest.

Secondly, Galatians 3:24. The KJV has the law of Moses as *"our schoolmaster unto Christ"*. A more proper translation of verse 24 reveals the Mosaic Law as a guardian, custodian, or guide. According to BDAG[118] 748 s.v. παιδαγωγός, "the man, usually a slave…whose duty it was to conduct a boy or youth…to and from school and to superintend his conduct generally; he was not a 'teacher' (despite the present meaning of the derivative 'pedagogue'…When the young man became of age, the guardian was no longer needed." If one neglects the context of this verse, it's easy to think the law being your schoolmaster and mine, leading us to faith in Christ. But context shows us a former Jewish Pharisee teaching people who want to live as Jews the futility of that desire.

Verse 19 reveals why the law was given - *It was added because of transgressions until the Seed to whom the promise was made would come.* Further, *Before this faith*

---

[118] Frederick W. Danker, Walter Bauer, *A Greek-English Lexicon of the New Testament and other Early Christian Literature.*

came, we were confined under the law, imprisoned until the coming faith was revealed. The law, then, was our guardian until Christ, so that we could be justified by faith. But since that faith has come, we are no longer under a guardian, for you are all sons of God through faith in Christ Jesus. (Galatians 3:23-26) Still further, *Now I say that as long as the heir is a child, he differs in no way from a slave, though he is the owner of everything. Instead, he is under guardians and stewards until the time set by his father. In the same way we also, when we were children, were in slavery under the elemental forces of the world.* (Galatians 4:1-3)

The Jewish people were kept by the law, given to them in covenant, to keep them separate from the rest of the peoples of the world. This was to keep that which was prophesied about the Messiah. When He came and established the New Covenant, slaves (to the law and elemental forces of the world) were set free by faith in Christ. *The Law and the Prophets were UNTIL John.* (Matthew 11:13; Luke 16:16.) The Law of Moses, as law functioning in covenant context, is over; was ended when the New Covenant was established. John came declaring what Christ was bringing about, a new kingdom which was spiritual not temporal, was eternal not temporary. The apostle John tells us, *for the law was given through Moses, grace and truth came through Jesus Christ* (John 1:17). This is the same message throughout – the Mosaic Law was for a time and space, given to a specific people until the promised Seed came.

Shane Kastler points out the difference in how these two Baptists confessions speak of the role of Mosaic Law in the life of the believer:

> Another striking difference between the two confessions is the use of language that speaks of the Law "binding" the Christian. Section nineteen of the

1689 Confession says this: "Although true believers be not under the law as a covenant of works, to be thereby justified or condemned, yet it is of great use to them as well as to others, in that **as a rule of life**, informing them of the will of God and their duty, **it directs and binds them** to walk accordingly." (emphasis added) And again, under the heading "Moral Law" the 1689 Confession says: "**The moral law doth for ever bind all**, as well justified persons as others, to the obedience thereof." (emphasis added) Regarding the Sabbath, the 1689 Confession says: "In His Word, by a positive, moral, and perpetual commandment **binding all men in all ages**, He has particularly appointed one day in seven, for a Sabbath, to be kept holy unto him." (emphasis added)[119]

The 1644 LBC makes no mention of Aquinas' theory of Moral Law. It makes no mention of any Mosaic Law being the rule for godly life. In the preface, it does proclaim belief in "all things that are written in the Law and the Prophets." Kastler poses this question: "Does a regenerate believer, who is indwelled by the Holy Spirit, need the Law of Moses to "bind" their conduct?"[120] Why would those with the new heart and the Holy Spirit indwelling them need to be whipped by the Mosaic Law? Where in Scripture do we see this taught?

In contrast to the 1689 LBC's use of Mosaic Law as the rule of life, the 1644 LCB says this:

All believers are a holy and sanctified people, and that sanctification is a spiritual grace of the new

---

[119] Kastler, Part Two.
[120] Ibid.

covenant, and an effect of the love of God manifested in the soul, whereby the believer presseth after a heavenly and evangelical obedience to all the commands, which Christ as head and king in His new covenant hath prescribed to them.[121]

Kastler observes, "This focus on the regenerate nature of a Christian's obedience to Christ rather than a "binding" of the Law of Moses is much more in line with Christian spirit and practice."[122] This brother goes on to observe that the 1644 LBC "and 1689 London Baptist Confessions of Faith are both man-made documents. Both contain glorious truths; yet both could also contain genuine errors. They, like all man-made writings, must always be judged by their adherence to the Scriptures. For it is Scripture that we cling to. A doctrinal statement might help explain those glorious Scriptures but they can never replace them. And on the issue of the "terrors of the Law" the 1646 gets it right and the 1689 gets it wrong. The Law is not necessary to the preaching of the gospel. The only thing necessary to the preaching of the gospel is the gospel. Jesus Christ and Him crucified."[123]

> The Law is a whip; but the sinner is a dead horse. And you can beat the dead horse all day long with the whip and do nothing but bruise his corpse. The gospel, on the other hand, can bring that corpse to LIFE! The gospel can give him a new heart. And the gospel can reveal that in fact that dead horse was no horse at all......he was a sheep that just hadn't been found yet. The Law didn't save him; and Moses didn't find him. The gospel saved him because Jesus found him. The Law had a purpose and that purpose has

---

[121] 1644 LBC, Article XXIX.
[122] Kastler, Part Two.
[123] Kastler, Part Three.

been fulfilled. Now, Hallelujah! Light has come! And that light is Jesus Christ.[124]

The account in Acts 15 shed further light on this matter. The problem addressed by the council in Acts 15 was two-fold. Converted Jews had begun teaching everyone that 1.) salvation and 2.) life was according to the custom and law of Moses.

Vs 1 *Some men came down from Judea and began to teach the brothers: "Unless you are circumcised according to the custom prescribed by Moses, you cannot be saved!"*

Vs 5 *But some of the believers from the party of the Pharisees stood up and said, "It is necessary to circumcise them and to command them to keep the law of Moses!"*

The matter of salvation dealt with primarily by Peter, a converted Jew himself. In verse 9 he noted, *"He (God) made no distinction between us and them, cleansing their hearts by faith."* No circumcision or any other religious rite – faith in the Son of God is what saves sinners, whether Jew or Gentile.

The matter of life lived before God in the New Covenant was dealt with by the letter sent out, which was previewed in verses 19 & 20.

Acts 15:19-20 *"Therefore, in my judgment, we should not cause difficulties for those among the Gentiles who turn to God, but instead we should write to them to abstain from things polluted by idols, from sexual immorality, from eating anything that has been strangled, and from blood."*

The apostolic instructions for life in the New Covenant were not commands for them to keep the law of Moses. They gave

---

[124] Kastler, Part Three.

instruction on everyday things that they encountered in life. The dietary restrictions reflect what God told Noah. When Jesus was unveiling His kingdom, He taught a new ethic, life based on having a humble heart, loving God and neighbor, seeking heavenly rather than earthly wealth. When the Apostles later wrote about this topic (Romans 14, 1 Corinthians, James, 1 & 2 Peter, etc.), the teaching has roots in the Old Testament but is interpreted and applied differently. Rather than a sexual pervert being killed, he is thrown out of the assembly of saints until he repents. Rather than being forced by the sword to carry another's burden, the Christian seeks to serve his fellow man by bearing his burdens – and in so doing, fulfilling the Law of Christ.

New Covenant Requires New Law

1 Corinthians 9:19-21 *Although I am a free man and not anyone's slave, I have made myself a slave to everyone, in order to win more people. To the Jews I became like a Jew, to win Jews; to those under the law, like one under the law — though I myself am not under the law — to win those under the law. To those who are without that law, like one without the law — not being without God's law but **within Christ's law** — to win those without the law.*

Then observe: Paul described himself as not under the Jewish law (Mosaic) but he would ACT like he was, in order not to offend them. Then he said he would ACT like those who do not have that law (Gentiles) so it would not be a stumbling block.

And Paul said that he was not without God's law but within Christ's law. This shows that the law given to Moses is no longer God's law, but the law of Christ is now God's law.

This lines up with this:

Hebrews 7:11-12 *If then, perfection came through the Levitical priesthood (for under it the people received the law), what further need was there for another priest to appear, said to be in the order of Melchizedek and not in the order of Aaron? For* **when there is a change of the priesthood, there must be a change of law as well.**

The New Covenant has a new priesthood, which requires a new law. The New Covenant has different entry requirements than did the Old Covenant. Faith in God was not required to enter the Mosaic Covenant - obedience to a few religious rites were all that was required. New birth which brings faith in Christ is required to enter into the New Covenant - the flesh profits nothing! Shadows were fulfilled in the substance, which is Christ.

The 1644 LBC has no conflict with Scripture on this topic – it is largely silent on it. The 1689 LBC has much conflict with Scripture on this topic, having copied so much from the paedobaptists.

It seems clear from history that the authors of the 1644 LBC made free use of material from paedobaptists, General Baptists, and Anabaptists without polluting their biblical doctrine with any errors from those groups. It seems just as clear that the authors of the 1689 LBC made free use of material from paedobaptists alone, with obvious influence on this second generation of Particular Baptists.

6. Conclusion

If we put our hope and build our theology on what men say, we will be led astray and disappointed. The Bible is the only sure foundation for our system of theology – our view of God. A complex system will tend to fascinate many with its varied details, seemingly providing clarity – but, in truth – clouding the minds of those who accept it by allowing them to think understand things that they do not. They simply have a system written by men that induces them to think so.

This is the cage in which the papist cult holds its subjects. This is the cage in which the state-church and the paedobaptists hold their members.

It is man's natural condition to want to understand things – a God-given curiosity to comprehend our world and all that's in it. The danger comes when we expect this innate curiosity to be able to comprehend everything we read in Scripture. A read of any book in the Bible will have us wanting to know more about myriad things than what our God has pleased to reveal to us. If we get comfortable hypothesizing about what's not in the Bible, we will end up building a system of theology built on "good and necessary inference" rather than on the clear things found in Scripture. I call this "White Space Theology" – getting your theology from the white spaces between the words in the Bible.

History is replete with records of men building up systems of theology with straw – all the cults have done this. But so have the Reformed folk who build their systems on the "Covenant of Works" with Adam and a "Covenant of Grace" that is not the New Covenant.

Compounding this problem is the harsh reality that no man is completely pure in his motives. Each of us is prone to make changes in our world-view and theological system for pragmatic reasons. We are prone to value life and stuff too much and when those are threatened, we can be coerced and induced to make a small change here or there to relieve the pressure, mitigate the risk.

I see that the men who wrote both of the confessions in view in this book made changes for pragmatic reasons. The difference between the 1644 LBC and the 1689 LBC in this regard is that small changes were made to the 1st LBC in response to harassment by Presbyterians while the foundation used by the 2nd LBC was pragmatic from the beginning. The preface to that confession and many of its advocates admit this, though they dare not call it pragmatism. They call it "unification, restoration, and public vindication" and similar things. Samuel Renihan also said, "By confessing the exact same doctrine of the covenant of grace, dogmatically, the Particular Baptists intentionally placed themselves within Reformed covenantalism."[125] I have to ask myself, "Why is it important for current day Baptists to embrace this placement as a goal?" Is not the Bible our only guide for life and godliness?

When I labor in reading a lengthy religious document, such as the Westminster or 2nd London Baptist confessions, I admit Proverb 10:19 comes to mind: *"When there are many words, sin is unavoidable, but the one who controls his lips is wise."* In contrast, the concise simplicity of the 1644 LBC is refreshing. While the WCF and 1689 LBC each have much good content with which any child of God would quickly agree, the sad fact is men who advocate each of those confessions tend to make the "good and necessarily inferred" doctrines non-negotiable. When I was in elder training in a 1689 LBC congregation, I made it known I did not see a

---

[125] Samuel Renihan, p. 148.

"Christian Sabbath" as described in that confession. My mentor mentioned another elder who was most serious about following that confession and asked me if I could serve with him. I replied that I could serve with him, as I do not consider that day to be something to divide over; but I did think the other man would not serve with me, for that day is something to divide over in his mind. My mentor paused for a minute and then told me he thought I was right. There is no "Christian Sabbath" mentioned in Scripture. There is freedom to consider all days alike. Why would a made-up day be something to divide over?

The same thing happens with the "Covenant of Works" that is in the WCF and 1689 LBC - but not found in Scripture. We have to imagine it's there because our system of theology requires it. Why do its advocates work so hard to explain it and pretend it's clearly obvious? Adam being the federal head of all mankind would be the only such head in the Bible without a covenant, if there were no covenant with Adam. I see a simple one-way covenant in which God has decreed that all who are in Adam are, by nature, children of wrath. There is no promise of eternal life offered Adam if he kept himself from the tree of knowledge. There was the stark promise of death if he did not. Since the Fall was decreed by God, we can see Adam's sin was unavoidable, same as Judas' betrayal of Jesus. There is no good that comes out of hypothesizing what's not in Scripture. Just as the papist's traditions take on the status of Scripture over time, these inferred doctrines take on too much weight and become the "hill to die on" in our systems if theology. This should not be so.

I say again, all of the confessions mentioned in this book have much good in them, discussing several doctrines that are important to the New Covenant people of God. At the same time, none of these confessions were intended nor suitable for use in binding the consciences of those whom Christ has redeemed.

Lastly, I think it helpful to bear in the mind the reason for these confessions being written: to convince the state-church that these various congregations were not a political threat. Over the years, men have determined these confessions are to serve as doctrinal statements that members are to agree with and elders must subscribe to. In this model, we have to grapple with the human condition: the longer a document, the more varied its topics, the more people are likely to find something they disagree with. Since the assembly holds to the document as its summary of Christian faith, each member must choose to ignore his conscience or be known as a trouble-maker. A confession or doctrinal statement that is intended to be the basis for the gathering of a given congregation should be short and basic enough for each child of God to honestly embrace it. Yes, make your doctrinal statement clear about your stance on critical doctrines: salvation, ecclesiology, baptism, etc.; but don't burden the saints with a hundred pages or more.

Let our focus be on the gospel, and the love God poured out into our souls so we love one another as we should rather that fight over lesser things.

Appendix 1 – The Anabaptist Connection[126]

PTS Journal, Issue 1 – Nov 2014

The Swiss and South-German Anabaptists: Misjudged Heroes of the Reformation

Perhaps some today will be surprised that a sincere, objective investigation of sixteenth-century Anabaptists[127] will uncover significant non-soteriological commonalities existing between New Covenant Theology proponents and the Swiss and South German Anabaptists. Since the earliest days of the Reformation, the Anabaptists have largely been characterized as theological radicals and heretics. William Estep rightly observes: "Perhaps there is no group within Christian history that has been judged as unfairly as the Anabaptists of the sixteenth century."[128] Relying upon the

---

[126] Excerpts from: Zachary S. Maxcey, *Historical Forerunners of New Covenant Theology*

[127] Anabaptists, meaning "re-baptizers," comes from the combination of the Greek words ana ("again") and baptizō ("baptize").

[128] William R. Estep, *The Anabaptist Story: An Introduction to Sixteenth-Century Anabaptism* (Grand Rapids, MI: William B. Eerdmans Publishing Co., 1963; reprint 1975, 1996), 1. I highly encourage New Covenant believers of all denominations, backgrounds, and ages to read Estep's Anabaptist Story for three reasons. First, it is important to educate believers that not all of the Anabaptists were radicals or heretics. Many sixteenth-century Anabaptists were in fact orthodox in their beliefs, especially on the nature of the church. Historians have largely misjudged them, preferring to highlight the Münsterites or the Inspirationists as typical representatives of mainstream Anabaptism. Second, many Anabaptist beliefs such as believer's baptism and the regenerate nature of the Church serve as foundational distinctives of the Baptist movement, both in its Particular and General forms. Third, there appears to be a relationship, both historical and doctrinal, between evangelical Anabaptism and many different Christian groups such as the English Separatists, the English and American Baptists, and advocates of New Covenant Theology.

biased secondary accounts of the Catholic Church and magisterial reformers,[129] historians have largely misjudged them, highlighting instead the Rationalists,[130] Inspirationists,[131] and Münsterites[132] as typical representatives of mainstream Anabaptism.[133]

---

[129] The 'magisterial' reformers were the more prominent members of the Protestant Reformation, such as Martin Luther, Ulrich Zwingli, Philip Melancthon, Heinrich Bullinger, John Calvin, John Knox, and others. For examples of the magisterial response to the sixteenth-century Anabaptists, see John Calvin, *Treatises against the Anabaptists and against the Libertines*, trans. Benjamin W. Farley (Grand Rapids, MI: Baker Book, 1982) and John S. Oyer, Lutheran Reformers against Anabaptists (Paris, AR: Baptist Standard Bearer, 1964).

[130] See Estep, *The Anabaptist Story*, 23. He writes, "The rationalists, as the term implies, put primary emphasis on the place of reason in interpreting the Scriptures. For the most part the evangelical rationalists were antitrinitarian, but they were antitrinitarian because they were rationalists and not the reverse. Reason, therefore, and not Scripture or special revelation became for them the source of ultimate authority."

[131] See Estep, *The Anabaptist Story*, 22. Estep writes, "For the inspirationists the Spirit took precedence over the Bible. Thus the immediate illumination of the Spirit became the norm for the inspirationist's program of reform. The Zwickau prophets, Nicolaus Storch, and Thomas Münzter, claimed special revelation, as did later inspirationists." In general, the Inspirationist Anabaptists belittled the role of the Holy Scriptures in the life of a believer. Instead, they gave preeminence to the "guiding" role of the Holy Spirit, thus pitting the Spirit against His Word. This theologically-perilous and unbiblical approach allowed Inspirationist Anabaptists to be guided by their "spiritual" experiences rather than the Word of God. It goes without saying that the Holy Spirit never operates in a manner that contradicts the very Scriptures that He inspired.

[132] The Münsterites were radical members of the Anabaptist movement, whose infamous notoriety stems from the violent over-realized eschatology which they espoused. This eschatology eventually resulted in the Münster Rebellion which was quickly and decisively crushed by the leaders of medieval Germany in 1535 A.D.

[133] Two factors primarily contribute to the misrepresentation of the Anabaptists. First, the more fringe elements of the Anabaptist movement, such as the Münsterites or the Inspirationists, have often been highlighted as the typical representatives of mainstream Anabaptism. For

Anabaptist Teachings regarding the Scriptures

The first strong commonality which exists between New Covenant Theology and the Swiss and South German strains of Anabaptism involves the doctrine and interpretation of Scripture. First, like most Protestant Reformers, these Anabaptists employed the principle of sola Scriptura[134].

Estep notes the following:

> The one sure touchstone of the Reformation and clear line of demarcation between Roman Catholics and Reformers was the authority of the Scriptures. **Within the Reformation no group took more seriously the principle of sola Scriptura in matters of doctrine and discipline than did the true Anabaptists.** In this regard the Reformation stance of the Anabaptists is unequivocal. The authoritative position of the Scriptures among the sixteenth-century Anabaptists was apparent from the beginning. **The Bible became and remained for them the supreme judicature by which all human opinions were to be tried**[135] [emphasis mine].

Second, like other Reformers, they advocated the study of the Scriptures in their original languages, Greek, Hebrew,

---

the second, see Estep, The Anabaptist Story, 1. Historical accounts frequently rely "heavily upon the highly partisan and quite unreliable accounts of sixteenth-century Anabaptism in the writings of Ulrich Zwingli, Justus Menius, Heinrich Bullinger, and Christoph Fischer, to say nothing of the milder but just as erroneous accounts of Martin Luther and Philip Melanchthon."

[134] *Sola Scriptura* is a Latin phrase, meaning "by the Scriptures alone," which has served as a prominent rallying cry for Protestant theologians since the days of the Reformation. Sola Scriptura was used by Protestants to indicate that the Scriptures are the sole authority of faith and practice for the Christian.

[135] Estep, *The Anabaptist Story*, 190

and Aramaic. Third, the "Swiss and South German Anabaptists" considered "the New Testament, in particular the life and teachings of Christ" to be "the final authority for the Christian life and the faith and order of the church.[136]"

Concerning Hübmaier, Estep writes: "...Hübmaier...did honestly attempt to discover what the Scriptures taught and to exegete them faithfully. It is also evident that the New Testament became for him the sole authority for the Christian life and the life of the church."[137] Fourth, mainstream Anabaptists interpreted the Scriptures with a Christocentric hermeneutic. For example, Estep writes, "While they tended to interpret the Scriptures in a literal sense, they were Christocentric. It was Christ who in the actual formulation of the faith became the ultimate authority to which they appealed."[138] Fifth, they ought to interpret the Old Testament Scriptures in the light of the New Testament. Estep states:

Although they did not reject the Old Testament in a Marcionite fashion, **it was never allowed to take precedence over the New Testament or to become normative for the Christian faith.** Theirs was a New Testament hermeneutic that assumed a progression in the biblical revelation that culminated in the Christ-event. **Therefore, the Old Testament, although useful and often quoted, could never stand alone, unqualified by the New Testament** [emphasis mine].[139]

---

[136] Estep, *The Anabaptist Story*, 22
[137] Ibid., 97. See also Bergsten, Balthasar Hübmaier, 275. Bergsten writes, "When the Anabaptists rejected infant baptism, they were acting in accordance with Zwingli's original understanding of Scripture. But since Zwingli was not prepared to draw this conclusion from the New Testamnt, he [Hübmaier] felt obliged to change his hermeneutics."
[138] Ibid., 22.
[139] Estep, *The Anabaptist Story*, 22

Elsewhere, he writes concerning Pilgram Marpeck's hermeneutic:

> Marpeck's most creative contribution to Anabaptist thought was his view of the Scriptures. While holding the Scriptures to be the Word of God, he made a distinction between the purpose of the Old Testament and that of the New. As the foundation must be distinguished from the house, the Old Testament must be distinguished from the New. **The New Testament was centered in Jesus Christ and alone was authoritative for the Brethren. To hold that the Old Testament was equally authoritative for the Christian was to abolish the distinction between the two. Failure to distinguish between the Old and New Testaments leads to the most dire consequences**. Marpeck attributed the peasants' revolt, Zwingli's death, and the excesses of the Münsterites to this cause. Making the Old Testament normative for the Christian life is to follow the Scriptures only in part. In Marpeck's eyes the pope, Luther, Zwingli, and the 'false Anabaptists' were all guilty of this fundamental error [emphasis mine].[140]

Anabaptist Views regarding Baptism and the Nature of the Church

The second similarity between New Covenant Theology and the Swiss and South German strains of Anabaptism involves the practice of believer's baptism. Their study of the Scriptures in the original languages, coupled with the principle of sola Scriptura, led Anabaptists to reject

---

[140] Ibid, 126

paedobaptism[141] in favor of believer's baptism. Estep correctly notes, "Believer's baptism was for the Anabaptists the logical implementation of the Reformation principle of sola Scriptura. Almost as soon as the Anabaptist movement could be distinguished within the context of the Reformation itself, believers' baptism became the major issue."[142] Later, he succinctly summarizes the typical Anabaptist view of baptism:

> In opposition to the usual arguments for infant baptism the Brethren set forth their position, underscoring the basic insights of Anabaptism. *First, the nature of baptism rules out the possibility of infant baptism.* New Testament baptism requires prior conviction for, and repentance of sin, and faith in Christ. Baptism is viewed as a symbol of initiation into the church and sign of the new life which the believer has in Christ. "In other words, baptism is to be administered only after receiving the Holy Spirit; and children, though they are not necessarily condemned, do not have the Holy Spirit."
>
> *Second, baptism is a symbol and not a sacrament. It has no meaning where faith in Christ is absent. Third, Christ has set for us an example through his own baptism. Fourth, through the Great Commission, he has explicitly commanded us to teach and baptize. Fifth, baptism is not analogous to circumcision* [emphasis mine].[143]

The Anabaptist acceptance and practice of believer's baptism led to a new, distinctive view of the Church, which

---

[141] Again, paedobaptism is a theological term used to describe the practice of infant baptism.

[142] Estep, *The Anabaptist Story*, 201.

[143] Ibid, 206

fundamentally differed from that of the Roman Catholics and magisterial Reformers. Because they believed that baptism was only for committed, confessing believers, the Anabaptists resultantly believed that the New Testament Church is a body composed solely of regenerate believers who had identified with the Lord Jesus Christ in believer's baptism. Estep describes Hübmaier's view regarding the nature of the true church:

> The first mark of the true church, according to Hübmaier, is regeneration. Regeneration must precede membership. *Of course, in Anabaptist thought there can be no scriptural baptism without the prior experience of regeneration, and no church membership without baptism.* It, therefore, follows that regeneration must be an accomplished fact before one is enrolled in the visible church [emphasis mine].[144]

New Covenant Theology adherents certainly agree with the Swiss and South German Anabaptists regarding the practice of believer's baptism and the teaching that the Church is a body composed solely of regenerate believers who have identified with the Lord Jesus Christ in believer's baptism. These significant commonalities indicate a relationship between the Swiss and South German Anabaptists and many other Christian groups such as the English Separatists, the English and American Baptists, and advocates of New Covenant Theology.

The Relationship between the Anabaptists and First-Generation Seventeenth-Century English Particular Baptists

---

[144] Estep, *The Anabaptist Story*, 245

Although the Anabaptist movement originated in Zürich, Switzerland, it quickly spread into such areas as Germany and Holland. Under the guidance of Menno Simons, a prominent and instrumental Dutch Anabaptist, the movement thrived and became firmly entrenched in Dutch territory. Moreover, Holland served as the predominant fountainhead of Reformation thought, which included Anabaptist theology, into medieval England. B. R. White confirms the presence of Anabaptists in England as early as the reign of Henry VIII (1509 – 1547): "Long before John Smyth [1570 – 1612] and Thomas Helwys [1575 – 1616] there had been 'Anabaptists' (that is, 're-baptizers') in England. Although Henry VIII had caught a few and burned some, most, if not all, of these had been foreigners."[145]

Although most historians will concede that there was an Anabaptist presence in medieval England, few are willing to argue in favor of a relationship between the Anabaptists and the first-generation English Particular Baptists. Estep describes this unwillingness: "The relationship of continental Anabaptism to early English Baptist has long been subject to debate. However, in recent years it seems to be the vogue to discredit any viewpoint that posits an Anabaptist-Baptist historical relation."[146] Representing this recent approach, White argues against such:

> It is certainly more plausible to argue for the likelihood of influence from some Anabaptists upon seventeenth-century English Baptist beginnings than it is from Anabaptism upon the earlier Separatists. Even so, it should be noted that two careful studies seeking to estimate the influence of Anabaptism

---

[145] B. R. White, *The English Baptists of the 17TH Century* (Didcot, England: The Baptist Historical Society, 1996), 15.
[146] Estep, *The Anabaptist Story*, 271.

upon both General and Calvinistic Baptists origins found that no significant influence could be decisively proved.[147]

Even Estep, who is favorable to the Anabaptists, denies a direct relationship between the Anabaptists and the first-generation English Particular Baptists. He writes, "To claim that Baptists…are **direct** descendants of the Anabaptists is to assume that similarity of belief proves **causal** connections. Such relationship is assumed from something other than historical evidence. However, this is not to deny the pervasive **influence** of sixteenth-century Anabaptism upon succeeding generations but to point up the task of the historian [**emphasis mine**]."[148]

The event whereby the first-generation[149] seventeenth-century English Particular Baptists both surfaced historically and asserted themselves theologically was the publication of the 1644 First London Baptist Confession (FLBC). White notes, "The Calvinistic Baptists first appeared as a self-conscious group with the publication of their Confession in London in 1644."[150] The vast majority of the 1644 FLBC is derived from the 1596 True Confession of Faith (TCF), a Congregationalist confession authored by Francis Johnson, thus indicating that "the basic orientation of the Particular

---

[147] White, *The English Baptists*, 17. See also Bergsten, Balthasar Hübmaier, 46. Bergsten states, "…Baptist scholars have frequently regarded him as the forerunner of Baptist and Free Church movements of more recent times. On this question, one can say that at the most Hübmaier can be regarded as a prototype of the Baptist movement. However, there can be no talk of a direct historical and doctrinal continuity between the reformer at Waldshut and his Baptist sympathizers of later times."

[148] Estep, *The Anabaptist Story*, 267.

[149] The first-generation seventeenth-century English Particular Baptists encompass the time period of ca. 1630-1660 A.D.

[150] White, *The English Baptists*, 59

Baptists clearly was and remained non-separatist Congregational Calvinist, and not Anabaptist."[151] Surely, if any influence existed between the Anabaptists and the first-generation Particular Baptists of England, such a relationship would be demonstrable from the 1644 First London Baptist Confession (FLBC). Does the Confession actually support a relationship? Indeed, it does. For example, Article XL of the 1644 FLBC significantly deviates from the 1596 TCF's understanding of believer's baptism:

> The way and manner of the dispensing of this Ordinance, the Scripture holds out to be dipping or plunging the whole body under water: it being a sign, must answer the thing signified, which are these: first, the washing the whole soul in the blood of Christ: Secondly, that interest the Saints have in the death, burial, and resurrection; thirdly, together with a confirmation of our faith, that as certainly as the body is buried under water, and rises again, so certainly shall the bodies of the Saints be raised by the power of Christ, in the day of the resurrection, to reign with Christ.... The word Baptize, signifying to dip under water, yet as with convenient garments both upon the administrator and subject with all modesty. Matt. 3:16; John 3:23; Acts 8:38; Rev. 1:5 & 7:14 with Heb. 10:22; Rom. 6:3, 4, 5; I Cor. 15:28, 29 [modern spelling mine].[152]

Glen Stassen states:

---

[151] Glen H. Stassen, "Anabaptist Influence in the Origin of the Particular Baptist," The Menonnite Quarterly 36:4 (1962): 324.

[152] The Confession of Faith of those Churches which are commonly (though falsely) called Anabaptists (London: 1644), Article XL [modern spelling and capitalization original].

The central motif of the Baptist innovation is an interpretation of baptism which is discontinuous not only from the Congregational doctrine of baptism, but from all the Congregational doctrines. The convictions which it presupposes are absent from Congregational thought....*The central conviction involved in the new interpretation of baptism is the concentration on the death, burial, and resurrection of Christ* [**emphasis mine**].[153]

How do we account for this significant difference between the 1596 TCF and the 1644 FLBC? Stassen convincingly demonstrates that the Christological emphasis in the 1644 FLBC's definition of baptism is strongly representative of Dutch Anabaptist thought. He writes:

> Menno Simons' *Foundation Book* exactly fulfills all the requirements for explaining every detail of the Baptist innovations....*The Foundation-Book* was likely to have been available to the Baptists, both because of its widespread distribution and because it was the book which shaped the basic doctrines of the Mennonites. The frequency with which it was republished is phenomenal. Its Dutch publication dates before 1640 are 1539, 1558, 1562, 1565, 1567, 1579 [2], 1583, 1613, 1616 and two undated editions published in German in 1575.... The overall emphases of the *Foundation Book* are strikingly similar to the emphases of the Baptist innovations. Menno stresses discipleship, repentance, faith, baptism, the Lord's Supper, Christ as Lord and example, along with an appeal to the magistracy. *The section on baptism is even more striking in its similarity to the core of the Baptist pattern. The emphases are almost identical. The order of*

---

[153] Stassen, "*Anabaptist Influence*," 337.

their presentation is almost identical. The Scripture passages which are mentioned are almost identical. The almost complete identity can be seen readily in the following outline which indicates in order the chief points and Scripture passages in Menno's and the Baptist's sections on baptism.... Then Menno succinctly states the significance of being baptized. Each aspect of the Baptist pattern appears, and the sequence is identical: The ordinance of the Lord, hearing, believing, professing faith, discipleship, death, burial, and resurrection with Christ. The Scripture Menno quotes is the same Scripture which the Baptists quote [**emphasis mine**].[154]

Although the Particular Baptists did officially distance themselves from the Anabaptist movement, this fact does not disprove a relationship between them and the Anabaptists with regard to the nature of the church and the Law of God for at least three reasons. First, Anabaptist theology, especially in its Dutch strain, entered medieval England through Holland. Second, the first-generation seventeenth-century Particular Baptists of England clearly held views regarding baptism and the nature of the church which were nearly identical to those of the Anabaptists. Third, the 1644 FLBC replicates many doctrinal explanations and theological emphases found in Menno Simons' *Foundation-Book*.

Issue 2 Feb 2014

---

[154] Glen H. Stassen, "Anabaptist Influence in the Origin of the Particular Baptist," The Menonnite Quarterly 36:4 (1962) 341-343.

The first-generation seventeenth century English Particular Baptists held a view of the divine[155] covenants which significantly differed from the Westminster Confession of Faith (WCF) and later English Particular Baptists. These men, especially John Spilsbery, Thomas Patient, Samuel Richardson, and Benjamin Cox, understood the 'covenant of grace' to be the New Covenant and its counterpart 'covenant of works' to be the Old Covenant. More specifically, these first-generation Particular Baptists of England described the 'covenant of grace,' that is, the New Covenant, as an absolute covenant, a gracious covenant of life, and a spiritual covenant. Contrastingly, they described the 'covenant of works' or Old Covenant with such terms as a conditional covenant, a covenant of circumcision, and a national covenant.

Like the Westminster Divines, first-generation seventeenth-century English Particular Baptists believed that the Scriptures set forth two covenants: a 'covenant of works' and a 'covenant of grace.' However, they understood the 'covenant of grace' to be the New Covenant, an absolute covenant, and the 'covenant of works' to be the Old Covenant, a conditional covenant. As Patient wrote: "Now if any please but to search these Scriptures [Heb. 8:6-7] it will appear that there [are] two real distinct Covenants or Testaments, the one of Grace, and the other of works, the one conditional, the other absolute."

The first-generation seventeenth century English Particular Baptists also approached the Old and New Covenants from a more redemptive-historical viewpoint than did their Westminster contemporaries. They recognized that the Old Covenant was abolished and replaced by the New Covenant.

---

[155] A divine covenant is a God-established, Sovereignly-imposed, solemn arrangement of stipulations, instituted in time, whereby the Lord Freely and graciously condescends to and communes with ungloriθied man.

This approach differs from the Westminster Divines and the second generation[156] seventeenth-century English Particular Baptists who viewed the Old and New Covenants as two distinct out workings of the one over-arching 'covenant of grace,' thus flattening the redemptive-historical distinctiveness of both covenants. Consider the following words from Spilsbery:

> And of the Scriptures speaking of the disannulling and abolishing the old Covenant, and making a new, is to be understood of the Period from Moses to Christ, and not of that from Abraham to Moses. This also in part I confess, but not the whole; because...the abolishing of the old Covenant or Testament, reached unto all the outward form of worship, under any type of shadow, by which the people professed their faith and obedience to God.[157]

Not only did Spilsbery teach that the Old Covenant was abolished and replaced by the New Covenant, but he also biblically defined the operative time period of the Old Covenant: "the Period from Moses to Christ, and not of that from Abraham to Moses."

Unlike their Westminster counterparts, the first-generation English Particular Baptists did not believe that the Ten Commandments constituted the transcovenantal moral law of God. Rather, they rightly understood that Christ as the Lawgiver of the New Covenant issued a new system of covenantal law, according to which all New Covenant believers must conform their lives. For example, Spilsbery states, "But as there is a new King, *so there must be a new Law,* and as a new covenant, so a new subject; a new Church

---

[156] The second generation seventeenth-century English Particular Baptists encompass the time period of ca. 1650-1690 A.D.
[157] Spilsbery, *Lawful Subject of Baptism*

must have a new state, and a new ordinance, a new commandment, so that as all things are become new, even so must all be of God, whose will is to be obeyed in whatsoever He commands, which is the only ground of all man's obedience" [**emphasis mine**][158] It is also likely that Benjamin Cox's description of New Covenant law in his Appendix to the 1646 FLBC is derived from the Anabaptists as well. Recall that the "Swiss and South German Anabaptists" considered "the New Testament, in particular the life and teachings of Christ" to be "the Final authority for the Christian life and the faith and order of the church."[159] In Article 9 of his appendix to the 1646 FLBC, Benjamin Cox describes how the law relates to the New Covenant believer:

> Though we that believe in Christ be not under the law, but under grace, Rom. 6:14; yet we know that we are not lawless, or left to lie without a rule; "*not without law to God, but under law to Christ*," I Cor. 9:21. The Gospel of Jesus Christ is a law, or commanding rule unto us; whereby, and in obedience where unto, we are taught to live soberly, righteously, and godly in this present world, Titus 2:11, 12; the directions of Christ in His evangelical word guiding us unto, and in this sober, righteous, and godly walking, I Tim. 1:10,11 [**emphasis mine**].[160]

He continues in Article X:

---

[158] Spilsbery, *Lawful Subjects of Baptism*, 1.

[159] Estep, The Anabaptist Story, 22

[160] Benjamin Cox, Appendix to the 1646 First London Baptist Confession of Faith – A More Full Declaration of the Faith and Judgment of Baptized Believers (London: 1646), Article IX. See also The First London Confession of Faith 1646 Edition with an Appendix by Benjamin Cox, reprint ed. with historical background in a preface by Gary D. Long (Charleston, SC: www.CreateSpace.com; an Amazon Co., 2004).

Though we be not now sent to the law as it was in the hand of Moses, to be commanded thereby, yet Christ in His Gospel teacheth and commandeth us to walk in the same way of righteousness and holiness that God by Moses did command the Israelites to walk in, all the commandments of the Second Table being still delivered unto us by Christ, and all the commandments of the First Table also (*as touching the life and spirit of them*) in this epitome or brief sum, "Thou shalt love the Lord thy God with all thine heart, etc.," Matt. 22:37, 38, 39, 40; Rom. 13:8, 9, 10 [**emphasis mine**].[161]

Although the first-generation seventeenth-century English Particular Baptists believed that the Decalogue applied to them as New Covenant believers, they did not believe that it applied to them in the same sense "as it was in the hand of Moses" but as it was "delivered" to them from Christ in the New Covenant.

Issue 3 – May 2015

It is evident that the second-generation seventeenth-century English Particular Baptists differed significantly from the first-generation seventeenth-century English Particular Baptists with regard to the Law of God. The writings of Nehemiah Cox, a second-generation English Particular Baptist and son of Benjamin Cox, strongly agree with the SLBC's definition of the Law of God. Cox understood God's Law to be both an "internal and subjective" law written upon the heart of Adam.[162] He described the law in the following manner: "The sum of this law was afterward given in ten

---

[161] Ibid, Article X.
[162] Nehemiah Cox, "*A Discourse of the Covenants.*" Cited in *Covenant Theology: From Adam to Christ*, ed. Ronald D. Miller, James M. Renihan, and Francisco Orozco (Palmdale, CA: Reformed Baptist Academic Press, 2005),43.

words [i.e. Ten Commandments] on Mount Sinai and yet more briefly by Christ who reduced it to two great commands respecting our duty both to God and our neighbor (Matthew 22:37-40)."[163] Thus, like the Westminster Divines, Nehemiah Cox believed that the Ten Commandments as God's transcovenantal moral law were written upon Man's heart at his creation.

As demonstrated by the SLBC, the second generation seventeenth-century English Particular Baptists clearly understood the 'covenant of works,' in a manner virtually identical to that of the WCF. Moreover, Nehemiah Cox, a second generation English Particular Baptist, not only described the so-called 'covenant of works' as a pre-fall covenant between God and Adam but also insisted that Adam would have secured for himself eternal life had he remained obedient to God.[164] The SLBC's explanation of the 'covenant of grace' constitutes a mediating view between the FLBC and WCF, as it was revealed "to Adam in the promise of salvation by the seed of the woman" (i.e. it unites all of redemptive history) yet its "full discovery...was completed in the New Testament" [i.e. the New Covenant].[165] As a result, the 'covenant of grace' of the 2LBC still flattens the redemptive-historical distinctions of the biblical covenants (e.g., consider the 1689 Federalist teaching that all Old Testament saints received the indwelling Holy Spirit prior to Pentecost, in light of such texts as John 7:38-39; 14:16-17; Luke 24:49; and Acts 1:4-5-8). In brief, such understandings significantly differ from the first-generation seventeenth century English Particular Baptists, such as John Spilsbery,

---

[163] Ibid.

[164] Cox, "A Discourse of the Covenants," 43-45

[165] 1689 Federalism (i.e. embodied in the SLBC) overwhelmingly rejects the Westminster Confession's presentation of the 'covenant of grace' as one covenant with multiple administrations. Instead, modern 1689 Federalists assert that the 2LBC's 'covenant of grace' is the New Covenant.

115

who equated without qualification the 'covenant of works' with the Mosaic Covenant and the 'covenant of grace' with the New Covenant.

Appendix 2 – A Tale of Two Sabbaths

Stuart Brogden

The Bible declares itself to be sufficient for life and godliness for those indwelt by the Holy Spirit. This is the concept behind the doctrine of *Sola Scriptura*. People who truly hold to this doctrine will not embrace dogma that cannot be clearly taught from God's Word. While there are myriad issues that divide denominations and churches from one another, one's view of the Sabbath appears to be one of major contention amongst those who embrace the idea of *Sola Scriptura*. Within this arena there is a coalition who herald the Puritan view of the Sabbath, which is recorded in the Westminster and Second London Baptist confessions. What follows is a comparison between the biblical description of the weekly Sabbath and the confessional views of Christian Sabbatarians, according to the Second London Baptist Confession in chapter 22. Let the reader decide if the Puritans and those confessions had it right or followed traditions of man.

Biblical Sabbath	"Christian Sabbath"
Every 7th day (Ex 16:27-30, Ex 20:8-11, 31:15, 35:2; Lev 23:3; Deut 5:14)	Para 7: Claims One day in Seven (Ex20:8). Changed from the last day of the week to the first day of the week (citing 1 Cor 16:1-2; Acts 20:7); claiming "Christian Sabbath" as the Biblical Sabbath was abolished (no Scripture citation).
Rest from all work (Ex 16:23, 25; 20:8-10; 35:2; Lev 23:3; Num 15:32; Deut 5:12-15; Jer 17:21)	Para 8: Rest from all things (Isaiah 58:13; Neh 13:15-22).
Remain in your dwelling (Ex 16:29; Lev 23:3)	Private and public worship are commanded (para 8; no Scripture citation)

It is a sign to the Israelite (Ex 31:13, 16, 17; Lev 24:8; 2 Chr 2:4; Neh 9:14; Ezek 20:12, 20)	
Death penalty for violating it, even minor activities such as picking up sticks (Ex 31:14-15; Num 15:32-36)	
No fires for cooking, Sabbath day meals were prepared the day before (Ex 35:3)	
Ceremonial bread, made in accordance with a strict formula, was presented (Lev 24:8; 1 Chr 9:32)	
Offerings – consisting of lambs, grain, and drink (Num 28:9, 10)	
Soldiers/priests guard the temple (2 Kings 11:5-12; 2 Chr 23:4-8)	
Gentiles not bound (Deut 5:15; Neh 10:31)	Para 7: Claims "law of nature … by Gods appointment" a "moral, and perpetual commandment, binding all men, in all ages" (no Scripture citation).
Prohibited from business (buying or selling) with Gentiles (Neh 10:31, 13:15-19)	
Gentiles invited to join with God's people and keep the Sabbath (Isaiah 56:1-7)	
Israel to keep the Sabbath (Isaiah 58:13)	
	Duties of necessity and mercy are permitted (para 8; Matt 12:1-13)
No bearing of burdens (Jer 17:21-27)	

Notes:

1. The Second London Baptist Confession (1689 LBC) cites Exodus 20:8 for setting the Sabbath one day in seven and for binding all men. That verse does not mention the frequency of the Sabbath; verses 10 & 11 both specify the 7th day, that day which ended the week for the Hebrew nation. Every 7th day, not one day in seven – that's the

consistent record in Scripture. Neither does that passage mention anyone other than national Israel as the subjects of this covenant and this specific command.

2. The 1689 LBC then claims 1 Cor 16:1-2 and Acts 20:7 as a record of God having changed the day of observing the Sabbath. Read the texts – narratives showing the practice of the new church on "the day after the Sabbath." No instruction or record of changing the Sabbath; no record of establishing the "Christian Sabbath" or abolishing the 7th day Sabbath, which continued on during the Lord's time on earth and the apostolic era.

3. Because of the death penalty for minor infractions of the Sabbath command to rest (as shown in Ex 31 & Num 15), it was common in Israel for the people to ask the religious leaders for clarification of what was permissible. This developed into the complex, legalistic list of rules that were infamous in the time of Christ.

4. The "holy convocation" mentioned in Lev 23:3 is widely considered to have been a call to prayer, praise, and instruction from the Word of God. But the biblical record (Ex 12; Lev 23; Num 28 & 29) shows a consistent requirement to cease work, with cooking meals being the only exception. There is the occasional mention of humbling one's self, making offerings to God, and the blowing of trumpets. Some of these convocations lasted several days or weeks. There is nothing in Scripture to indicate this was a weekly occurrence of prayer, praise, and preaching; although extra-biblical history does show the post-exile nation adopting the weekly synagogue practice that was well established by the time of Christ.

5. There are many special Sabbaths, such as the Day of Atonement (Lev 23:32) and the Sabbath year (Lev 25). This comparison is restricted to the weekly Sabbath.

6. Nehemiah 13:20-22 reveals the only passage in Scripture wherein Gentiles are told about the Sabbath, their merchants being warned to leave the Jews alone on the Sabbath so the Jews won't be led astray. Gentiles are not commanded by Nehemiah to keep the Sabbath.

7. In Matthew 12, there is no support for the Mosaic Law permitting acts of mercy. We have Jesus making note that Jewish men would violate their Sabbath to save an animal. Jesus summed up His announcement that He is Lord of/over the Sabbath by saying it was "lawful to do what is good on the Sabbath." Contrary to the Mosaic Law, Jesus didn't define "good" and there's nothing indicating He was revealing the true meaning of the Sabbath law; there is nothing in the Mosaic Law that provides for acts of mercy on the Sabbath. Jesus even said the Jews broke the Sabbath by circumcising on that day, because circumcision was more important.

8. There is not one Scripture cited by the 1689 LBC showing the weekly Sabbath being addressed to, defined for, imposed on, or required of anyone other than those under the rule of Moses. Nor is there any biblical record of Christians keeping the Sabbath.

Appendix 3 - The Decalogue Contrasted with The Law of Christ

Stuart L. Brogden

The Decalogue is tied to the Mosaic Covenant.

In four places in Scripture (listed below), the Decalogue is described as the Mosaic Covenant. While it is not the sum total of everything given to ethnic Israel (see Ex. 34:32), the Decalogue is certainly the Tablets of Testimony of that covenant (Ex. 25:16; 31:18, 32:15, 34:29).

Exodus 34:28 *Moses was there with the LORD 40 days and 40 nights; he did not eat bread or drink water.* ***He wrote the Ten Commandments, the words of the covenant****, on the* tablets.

Deuteronomy 4:12-13 *Then the LORD spoke to you from the fire. You kept hearing the sound of the words, but didn't see a form; there was only a voice.* ***He declared His covenant to you. He commanded you to follow the Ten Commandments, which He wrote on two stone tablets.***

1 Kings 8:20-21 *The LORD has fulfilled what He promised. I have taken the place of my father David, and I sit on the throne of Israel, as the LORD promised. I have built the temple for the name of Yahweh, the God of Israel. I have provided* ***a place there for the ark, where the LORD's covenant is*** *that He made with our ancestors when He brought them out of the land of Egypt.*

2 Chronicles 6:10-11 *So Yahweh has fulfilled what He promised. I have taken the place of my father David and I sit on the throne of Israel, as Yahweh promised. I have built the temple for the name of Yahweh, the God of Israel. I have put*

the ark there, where Yahweh's covenant is that He made *with the Israelites.*

There are **two versions of the Decalogue**, and they differ in ways not explained by textual variances. Which version is authoritative? Secondly, the Decalogue, being carved in stone tablets and called "the Ten Words" would not fit on stone tablets if all the words found in the Exodus 20 or Deuteronomy 5 versions were counted as these ten words. If you see the Decalogue as God's "Moral Law" how do you derive what that "moral law" is? Which version of the 4th word is authoritative?

Consider Exodus 20:5-6 (ESV) *You shall not bow down to them or serve them, for I the LORD your God am a jealous God,* **visiting the iniquity of the fathers on the children to the third and the fourth generation of those who hate me,** *but showing steadfast love to thousands of those who love me and keep my commandments.* Is this part of the "moral law" - being smack in the middle of both versions of the Decalogue? How do we conclude what words spoken by Moses were carved in stone? If the Decalogue is the eternal, unchanging moral law of God, why did YHWH repeal the vengeance found in Exodus 20:5 in Deuteronomy 24:16? *Fathers are not to be put to death for [their] children* **or children for [their] fathers; each person will be put to death for his own sin.**

The Law of Moses was given to National Israel, alone.

Deuteronomy 5:1-5 *Moses summoned all Israel and said to them,* "**Israel, listen to the statutes and ordinances I am proclaiming as you hear them today.** *Learn and follow them carefully.* **The LORD our God made a covenant with us at**

Horeb. He did not make this covenant with our fathers, but with all of us who are alive here today. The LORD spoke to you face to face from the fire on the mountain. At that time I was standing between the LORD and you to report the word of the LORD to you, because you were afraid of the fire and did not go up the mountain.

Deuteronomy 5:12-15 *Be careful to remember the Sabbath day, to* **keep it holy as the LORD your God has commanded you.** *You are to labor six days and do all your work, but the seventh day is a Sabbath to the LORD your God.* **You must not do any work**—*you, your son or daughter, your male or female slave, your ox or donkey, any of your livestock, or the foreigner who lives within your gates, so that your male and female slaves may rest as you do.* **Remember that you were a slave in the land of Egypt, and the LORD your God brought you out of there with a strong hand and an outstretched arm. That is why the LORD your God has commanded you to keep the Sabbath day.**

This reissuing of the covenant and law provided the historical context ethnic Israel needed to ground them in their identity with YHWH. They, not others, were His covenant people. This version of the 4th word aligns with the introduction, clearly showing this law was given, as part and parcel of the covenant, to only those who were on Mt. Horeb when YHWH gave the law and covenant to the infant nation of Israel. Moses makes it very clear that this law was not given to Abraham, Isaac, and Jacob, but to them who were on the mountain on that day.

Nehemiah 9:13-14 **You came down on Mount Sinai, and spoke to them** *from heaven.* **You gave them** *impartial ordinances, reliable instructions, and good statutes and* *commands.* **You revealed Your holy Sabbath to them, and** *gave them commands, statutes, and instruction through Your servant Moses.*

John 7:19 *Didn't Moses give you the law?*

John 8:17 *Even in your law it is written that the witness of two men is valid.*

Romans 9:4 *They are Israelites, and to them belong the adoption, the glory, the covenants, the giving of the law, the temple service, and the promises.*

In both Old and New Covenant passages, the law of Moses is described as being given to ethnic Israel; not to the world and not to the saints.

The Law of Moses is a unit, not divisible into different categories.

Galatians 3:10 *For all who rely on the works of the law are under a curse, because it is written: Everyone who does not continue doing everything written in the book of the law is cursed.*

Galatians 5:3 *Again I testify to every man who gets himself circumcised that he is obligated to keep the entire law.*

James 2:10 *For whoever keeps the entire law, yet fails in one point, is guilty of [breaking it] all.*

The law is consistently spoken of as a unit - keeping one point obligates one to keep every point; failing on one point is being guilty of the whole law. Every law given by God is moral, for He is pure morality. The covenant context reveals how and to whom His specific laws are to be kept. Those in Adam are bound to God's Universal Law (called the law of nature or law of conscience by some); those who were in the Mosaic community were bound to the Mosaic Law; those who are in Christ are bound by the Law of Christ. All of these laws have points in common for they all come from God.

Why the Law of Moses was given.

Romans 5:20 *The law came along to multiply the trespass.*

Galatians 3:19 *Why then was the law [given]?* ***It was added because of transgressions*** *until the Seed to whom the promise was made would come.*

Galatians 3:22-23 *But the Scripture has imprisoned everything under sin's power, so that the promise by faith in Jesus Christ might be given to those who believe.* ***Before this faith came, we were confined under the law, imprisoned until the coming faith was revealed.***

Romans 7:7 *What should we say then? Is the law sin? Absolutely not! On the contrary,* ***I would not have known sin if it were not for the law****. For example,* ***I would not have known what it is to covet if the law had not said, Do not covet.***

Many claim the law was given to restrain sin - I find that taught nowhere in Scripture. It provides the basis for punishing law-breakers, ***For the law produces wrath. And where there is no law, there is no transgression.*** (Romans 4:15.)

The Law of Moses was for a time.

Matthew 11:13 ***For all the prophets and the Law prophesied until John***;

125

Luke 16:16 **The Law and the Prophets were until John**; *since then, the good news of the kingdom of God has been proclaimed,*

When John came, as the herald of the promised Seed, the Law's prophetic purpose ended.

Romans 7:1 *Since I am speaking to those who understand law, brothers, are you unaware that* **the law has authority over someone as long as he lives**?

Romans 7:4 **Therefore, my brothers, you also were put to death in relation to the law** *through the [crucified] body of the Messiah, so that you may belong to another—to Him who was raised from the dead—that we may bear fruit for God.*

Romans 7:6 **But now we have been released from the law, since we have died to what held us**, *so that we may serve in the new way of the Spirit and not in the old letter of the law.*

Galatians 2:19 *For through the law* **I have died to the law, so that I might live for God.**

The Jews who were dead to Christ and alive to the law were under that law. Those Jews who were made alive in Christ were put to death in relation to the Law. They serve in the new and better way of the Spirit of God, not in the old letter that brought death. Paul goes so far (in Gal. 2) as to say that, in order to live for God, one must die to the law. This lines up with what he wrote in Romans 7 - and it aligns with other Scripture that says if you live by the law you must do all of it and will be cursed if you do not. Far better to die to the law and be alive in Christ!

Galatians 3:19 *Why then was the law [given]? It was added because of transgressions* **until the Seed to whom the promise was made would come.**

When the promised Seed came, the law as regulation ended - along with its covenant.

Galatians 3:22-26 *But the Scripture has imprisoned everything under sin's power, so that the promise by faith in Jesus Christ might be given to those who believe. Before this faith came, we were confined under the law, imprisoned until the coming faith was revealed.* **The law, then, was our guardian until Christ**, *so that we could be justified by faith. But* **since that faith has come, we are no longer under a guardian**, *for you are all sons of God through faith in Christ Jesus.*

The law was the guardian (not tutor or schoolmaster as some translations say - this is a modern definition which was not in use when Paul wrote this passage) for national Israel. The law kept, guarded Israel until the promised Seed came. When Christ came, the law ceased in that function as well. No longer prophetic, no longer regulation, no longer guardian. Something new has come!

The Law of Moses was abolished.

Romans 10:4 *For* **Christ is the end of the law** *for righteousness* **to everyone who believes.** The law was ended, set aside as law, for all who believe in Christ.

Ephesians 2:15 *He* **made of no effect the law consisting of commands and expressed in regulations**, *so that He might create in Himself one new man from the two, resulting in peace.*

2 Corinthians 3:11 *For if what* **was fading away** *was glorious, what endures will be even more glorious.*

Appendix 3 – The Decalogue Contrasted with The Law of Christ

Here we see the Mosaic Law, inclusive of the commandments written on stone, was abolished, annulled, ended, set aside, fading away (Strong's G2673 - destroy, abolish). This is not the same word found in Matthew 5:17, which is G2647; they are similar. The law was abolished, destroyed as law (Eph. 2, 2 Cor. 3) but not destroyed as revelation.

Jesus fulfilled the law, which all throughout Matthew does not mean "confirmed" or "kept" but means filled up, complete; brought to its intended end. The word "fulfilled" (*pleroo*) is used 16 times in this gospel; by far the preponderance of the appearances of *pleroo* are 'eschatological.' By this is it meant not that they have reference to the Second Coming, but that from the Old Covenant perspective they represent a future work of God tied to a particular age (i.e. the New Covenant). The fulfillment has to do with how the Old Covenant prophetic word is taken up in the person and work of Christ. One example is: *When [Joseph] arose, he took the young Child and His mother by night and departed for Egypt, and was there until the death of Herod, that it might be fulfilled which was spoken by the Lord through the prophet, saying, 'Out of Egypt I called My Son.'* It is with this fulfillment in particular that we catch a glimpse of Matthew's vision with regard to the profound nature of Christ's fulfillment of prophecy. Throughout this gospel, "fulfillment" is part and parcel of the shadow/fulfillment process found throughout the redemptive story; it is not testimony of Jesus keeping the law.

***Keep* the law**. *tēreō* (5083): from *teros* (a watch; perhaps akin to <G2334> (*theoreo*)); to guard (from loss or injury, properly by keeping the eye upon.

***Fulfill* the law.** *plēroō* (4137): from <G4134> (*pleres*); to make replete, i.e. (literal) to cram (a net), level up (a hollow). As one author put it: "That which was empty, sketchy, has become filled up, filled out, and thereby glorified."

The New Covenant laws

We in the New Covenant are not without law; but we are not within the Law of Moses. New Covenant passages describe this new law as *the Spirit's law of life*, the *law of Christ*, *the perfect Law of Liberty*, and *the Royal law*. This law is based on the two great commandments, to love God and neighbor - not as taught by the Mosaic Law but as taught and modeled by the Lord Jesus, in light of the power of the Holy Spirit. As explained below in the section on hermeneutics, this Law of Christ is a principle rather than a list of legal requirements and prohibitions. It's given to a spiritual people, not a carnal people.

Romans 8:1-2 *Therefore, no condemnation now exists for those in Christ Jesus, because **the Spirit's law of life** in Christ Jesus has set you free from the law of sin and of death.*

Galatians 6:2 *Carry one another's burdens; in this way you will fulfill **the law of Christ.***

1 Corinthians 9:21 *To those who are without [that] law, like one without the law—not being without God's law but **within Christ's law**—to win those without the law.*

James 1:25 *But the one who looks intently into **the perfect law of freedom** and perseveres in it, and is not a forgetful hearer but one who does [good] works—this person will be blessed in what he does.*

James 2:8 *Indeed, **if you keep the royal law** prescribed in the Scripture, Love your neighbor as yourself, you are doing well.*

This phrase, *love your neighbor as yourself*, is the second great command, taken from Leviticus 19:18. It is the other side of the coin which also conveys the greatest command: Y*ou shall love the LORD your God with all your heart and with all your soul and with all your might,* cited from Deuteronomy 6:5. On these two commands, neither taken from the Decalogue, hang the Law and the prophets – all the scripture then in the hands of man. This shows us that while the Law of Moses is not our master, certain truths that apply to all of God's people are found in His books. Jesus draws out two and declares them to be supreme to the Old Covenant, the essence of the New Covenant – love for God and one another; love as defined and portrayed by Christ in the Bible, not as in the ancient Hebrew world or as our culture, which has deceitfully defined "love" these past few centuries.

Contrasting Old and New Covenant laws

As Moses went up into a mountain to **get the old Law**, so Christ went up into a mountain to **give the new Law** (Matt. 5-7). The old law was the ministry of death, chiseled on stone; the ministry of the Spirit is far more glorious. Unbelievers have a veil over their minds - this is removed only if they turn to Christ in faith. *Now the Lord is the Spirit, and where the Spirit of the Lord is, there is freedom. We all, with unveiled faces, are looking as in a mirror at the glory of the Lord and are being transformed into the same image from glory to glory; this is from the Lord who is the Spirit.*

(2 Cor. 3:7-17) Nowhere do we find the Mosaic Law tied to this transformation.

John 1:17 *for **the law was given through Moses, grace and truth came through Jesus Christ.*** Just as there is a distinct contrast between law and gospel, here John reveals a distinct contrast between law and grace & truth. The covenant given through Moses was a law-based covenant, with all the criminal sanctions for violations. The covenant made with the blood of Christ is a grace-based covenant, with forgiveness for sin and no legal code hanging over the heads of those within it.

In the Sermon on the Mount, Jesus contrasted the ethics of His kingdom with that of the kingdom of Israel, quoting two of the Ten Words exactly, showing how the law of His kingdom is a higher standard not found in the Mosaic Law. "*Do not murder*" does not teach "*love others as I have loved you;*" "*Do not commit adultery*" does not teach "*love your wife as Christ loved the church.*" "*Love your neighbor and hate your enemy*" was not part of the Decalogue, but it was taught in their law (Deut. 7:1-2) and prophets (Psalm 139:19-22) and displayed in the way ethnic Israel lived - as they applied the Levitical law (cities of refuge, Samaritans as "dogs", etc.).

The parable of the Good Samaritan shows that the Jews had the wrong idea of who their neighbors were - they thought only fellow Jews were their neighbors. That parable also showed how they hated their enemies, as the Pharisee crossed to the other side of the street to avoid the unclean person in the ditch. If the injured man had been a Jew, the Pharisee would have helped him; he wasn't a Jew, so he was a "dog" - an outsider and enemy of Israel. Jesus said, "*Love your enemies, pray for them;*" He was teaching that in His kingdom, everyone you come in contact with is your neighbor and we are to do good to all, especially those in the household of faith. There is a different mindset than in the Mosaic community; one based on love rather than a legal code.

Christ teaches those things which Moses did not. How could the Decalogue be our law if Jesus gave us a higher, better law?

Acts 15:5 *But some of the believers from the party of the Pharisees stood up and said, "**It is necessary to circumcise them and to command them to keep the law of Moses!**"* Acts 15:10 *Now then, **why are you testing God** by putting a yoke on the disciples' necks that neither our ancestors nor we have been able to bear?* The light yoke of Christ is light because Christ is the "lead ox" but also because there's a different load being pulled. Not the tablets of stone but the law of Christ. Telling saints they must keep the Law of Moses is testing God! This passage is not restricted to justification as the controversy was about justification and how Gentile Christians were to live. The charge from the Pharisees, the discussion, and the letter all reflect this larger scope.

2 Corinthians 5:14 *For **Christ's love compels us**.* Law keeping is not what gives us love nor the ability to obey; the love of Christ does this.

Romans 8:1-2 *Therefore, no condemnation now exists for those in Christ Jesus, because **the Spirit's law of life in Christ Jesus has set you free from the law of sin and of death.*** As explained below, I do not think either law mentioned in this passage is a legal code, but a principle. The principle of life is tied to faith, and law-keeping is not of faith (Gal. 3:12); the principle of sin and death is tied to unbelief.

Since Paul declared the law chiseled in letters on stone to be "*the ministry of death*" (2 Cor. 3) how can that law be the law of the New Covenant, wherein all is life? How can the Decalogue be for the saints when the Spirit's law of life in Christ has set us free from it?

How can the Decalogue be part of the Law of Christ when it is starkly contrasted with it in 1 Corinthians 9:19-21? *For **though I am free from all**, I have made myself a servant to all, that I might win more of them. **To the Jews I became as a Jew, in order to win Jews. To those under the law I became as one under the law (though not being myself under the law) that I might win those under the law. To those outside the law I became as one outside the law (not being outside the law of God but under the law of Christ) that I might win those outside the law.*** Paul described himself as being without - not having - the Law of Moses; he merely behaved as though he was under that law so his freedom would not distract Jews from his gospel. He made clear his true status in verse 21- not under the Law of Moses but under the law of Christ. How could the Law of Moses (its capstone - the Decalogue) be part of or equal to the law of Christ when Paul sets that against one another in several places?

Galatians 3:2-6 (ESV) *Let me ask you only this: Did you receive the Spirit by works of the law or by hearing with faith? Are you so foolish? **Having begun by the Spirit, are you now being perfected by the flesh?** Did you suffer so many things in vain — if indeed it was in vain? **Does he who supplies the Spirit to you and works miracles among you do so by works of the law, or by hearing with faith** — just as Abraham "believed God, and it was counted to him as* *righteousness"?* Having been given life by the Spirit, maturing in Christ is NOT by works of law-keeping!

Hebrews 7:11-13, 18, 19 *If then, perfection came through **the Levitical priesthood (for under it the people received the law)**, what further need was there for another priest to appear, said to be in the order of Melchizedek and not in the order of Aaron? **For when there is a change of the priesthood, there must be a change of law as well.** For the One these things are spoken about belonged to a different tribe. ... **So the previous command is annulled because it was weak and unprofitable (for the law perfected nothing)**, but a better hope is introduced, through which we draw near to God.* Law is tied to covenant. The Mosaic Law was based on the Mosaic Covenant, administered by the Levitical priesthood. When the New Covenant came, the priesthood changed - and this mandated a change of law as well. The law of the Old Covenant was annulled as law, it was not translated into the New Covenant as law. The Spirit provides a better hope, by which we draw near to God.

Hebrews 10:1 (ESV) *For since **the law has but a shadow of the good things to come** instead of the true form of these realities, **it can never**, by the same sacrifices that are continually offered every year, **make perfect those who draw near.*** The Law of Moses had its purpose in its time. It was unable to save and unable to make perfect anyone as **it was mere shadow while the substance is Christ** (Col. 2:17).

John 15:12 (ESV) ***This is my commandment, that you love one another as I have loved you****. John 15:17 (ESV) **These things I command you, so that you will love one another.*** This is the Law of Christ - the rule for Christian living is not the Law of Moses, not the "moral Law of God" as the Decalogue is called by man.

Romans 13:8 *Do not owe anyone anything, except to love one another, for* **the one who loves another has fulfilled the law.**

Romans 13:10 *Love does no wrong to a neighbor.* **Love, therefore, is the fulfillment of the law.**

Galatians 5:14 **For the entire law is fulfilled in one statement: Love your neighbor as yourself.**

There are some who claim Christians must live under the Decalogue as a rule of life or we will think murder is OK. Christians are indwelt by the Spirit of God and we have been shown that selfish anger at a brother is the same as murder, and we do not un-hinge the Old Testament from our theology. We read about how wicked murder is and see our anger at others is of the same sinful attitude. We read how we are to love one another as Christ loved us and see how great indeed the two Great Commandments are. We are not lawless; we are within the Law of Christ!

Great Commission: *Teaching them all I have commanded you.* Where did Jesus teach that His disciples are to keep the Decalogue? Jesus told His disciples the greatest commandment was to love God - something not taught in the Decalogue. He also told us the second greatest commandment is to love one another as He loved us - something not taught in the Decalogue.

How can the Decalogue be in the law of Christ when it doesn't command or teach us to LOVE? The Decalogue teaches what sin is.

Paul teaches that the Law is good and that it is the ministry of death. The best way to reconcile his statements is to see that the Law serves as revelation from God, and this is very good; it also serves as regulation for those under the law covenant, and this is very heavy. This is clearly seen in Romans 3:21 *But now,* ***apart from the law*** *[as regulation], God's righteousness has been revealed—attested by the Law and the Prophets [as revelation].*

One rule of hermeneutics that is very helpful.

Law exists in Scripture as Regulation and Revelation. John Owen recognized this, saying, "The law is taken two ways: 1. For the whole revelation of the mind and will of God ... and 2. For the covenant rule of perfect obedience."

Law as regulation is given in context of the covenant to which it belongs. Violations of law bring consequences, which are spelled out in that covenant.

There is no exception to this, in that laws with punishments do not spill out of their covenant. This is evidenced by the fact that people outside ethnic Israel were never told they had to obey the Mosaic Law; only covenant members were told this.

Since all of God's Word is Revelation, it is good for us if applied properly. This goes for law and narrative.

This is why a principle is seen in more than one law in more than one covenant - it's all from God. Don't confuse that with the papist fable of "trans-covenantal law."

A corollary is that "law" does not always refer to the Mosaic Law, the Decalogue, or to a codified list of legal requirements. In Romans 8:2 & 3 the word "law" is used three times: the Spirit's law of life, the law of sin and death, and the law. Paul normally refers to the entire Mosaic Law when "the law" is seen without any further description. "The law of sin" shows up in Romans 7 as well, in verse 23 & 24; in this passage this law cannot be the Mosaic Law, for it is contrasted with that law in the passage. This law of sin appears to be a principle, not a codified list of legal requirements or prohibitions. So in chapter 8, the law of sin and death would be the same principle - sin works death. It's a law in that nobody escapes; it's not a list of laws but a principle. I submit the Spirit's law of life is likewise a principle and not a list of laws. The construct is the same as the law of sin and is similar to our law of gravity - a principle. Context helps us determine meaning. Paul consistently teaches in Romans and Galatians that keeping the Mosaic Law is opposed to the spiritual walk we are called to. We, like Isaac, are children of promise, contrasted with children of slaves who were under the Mosaic Covenant (Galatians 4:21ff).

Summary

Man is naturally wired for works righteousness. Having a codified list of "Do"s and "Don't"s satisfies our natural desire to prove ourselves. This is not how we, who are **dead to the law and alive in Christ**, are to live - for *love does not keep records of wrongs* (1 Cor. 13:5). The Mosaic Law was not given as a rule for life for those indwelt by the Spirit of God. Christ has taught us and shown us how to love, He has given us His Spirit and His Word so we would not be left to figure it out on our own. And He has given us to one another so we can practice loving one another in spite of our differences and disagreements. May it please the Lord our God to continue to pour out His love and grace on us so we would shine as lights in this wicked world.

Appendix 3 – The Decalogue Contrasted with The Law of Christ

Appendix 4 – A Holy People

A Holy people.

1 Peter 2:9-10 *But **you are a chosen race, a royal priesthood, a holy nation, a people for His possession**, so that you may proclaim the praises of the One who called you out of darkness into His marvelous light. Once you were not a people, but now you are God's people; you had not received mercy, but now you have received mercy*. The testimony of Scripture is consistent – the redeemed people of God are made holy by being redeemed and we are to be holy in our all conduct.

1 Samuel 2:2 reminds us *No one is holy like the Lord, For there is none besides You, Nor is there any rock like our God.* In an absolute sense, our personal holiness cannot be compared with God's holiness. God alone is truly holy. Yet we are told be holy/set apart because YHWH is holy (1 Pet. 1:16). 1 Samuel 2:3 shows us how to pursue this holiness: *Talk no more so very proudly; Let no arrogance come from your mouth.* 1 Peter 1:13-15 provides more clarity: *be sober, and rest your hope fully upon the grace that is to be brought to you at the revelation of Jesus Christ; as obedient children, not conforming yourselves to the former lusts, as in your ignorance; but as He who called you is holy, you also be holy in all your conduct.* The source of our holiness is God – Peter said we are to be sober minded, resting fully on the grace of God. This is the foundation for what follows – obedient children not practicing the evil we did. Christian holiness is not based on keeping cultic religious rites; it's the product of being redeemed and sanctified by our Holy God.

Holy people – not holy days.

Colossians 2:16-17 *Therefore, don't let anyone judge you in regard to food and drink or in the matter of a festival or a new moon or a Sabbath day. These are a shadow of what was to come; the substance is the Messiah.*

Far too often debate about how to interpret this passage focuses on the phrase "Sabbath day," rather than seeking to understand the picture painted by the apostle. Countless times, the meaning of what we read in the New Testament can be rightly understood by having knowledge of the Old Testament. So it is with this lesson in Colossians 2:16-17.

The phrase "*festival or a new moon or a Sabbath day*" must be looked at, not merely the Sabbath day. Paul says "*these things*," referring to what was mentioned in verse 16 – food, drink, festivals, new moons, and Sabbath days. The phrase "*festival or a new moon or a Sabbath day*" shows up in 7 Old Covenant passages, provided below. Please read through them and do not be put off if the words are not in the same order as in Colossians 2 – the picture is the same.

1 Chronicles 23:30-32 *They are also to stand every morning to give thanks and praise to the LORD, and likewise in the evening. Whenever burnt offerings are offered to the LORD on **the Sabbaths, New Moons, and appointed festivals**, they are to do so regularly in the LORD's presence according to the number prescribed for them. They are to carry out their responsibilities for the tent of meeting, for the holy place, and for their relatives, the sons of Aaron, in the service of the LORD's temple.*

2 Chronicles 2:4 *Now I am building a temple for the name of Yahweh my God in order to dedicate it to Him for burning fragrant incense before Him, for displaying the rows of the bread of the Presence continuously, and for sacrificing burnt*

offerings for the morning and the evening, **the Sabbaths and the New Moons, and the appointed festivals** *of the LORD our God. This is ordained for Israel forever.*

2 Chronicles 8:12-13 *At that time Solomon offered burnt offerings to the LORD on the LORD's altar he had made in front of the portico. He followed the daily requirement for offerings according to the commandment of Moses for* **Sabbaths, New Moons, and the three annual appointed festivals***: the Festival of Unleavened Bread, the Festival of Weeks, and the Festival of Booths.*

2 Chronicles 31:2-3 *Hezekiah reestablished the divisions of the priests and Levites for the burnt offerings and fellowship offerings, for ministry, for giving thanks, and for praise in the gates of the camp of the LORD, each division corresponding to his service among the priests and Levites. The king contributed from his own possessions for the regular morning and evening burnt offerings, the burnt offerings of* **the Sabbaths, of the New Moons, and of the appointed feasts***, as written in the law of the LORD.*

Nehemiah 10:32-33 *We will impose the following commands on ourselves: To give an eighth of an ounce of silver yearly for the service of the house of our God: the bread displayed before the LORD, the daily grain offering, the regular burnt offering,* **the Sabbath and New Moon offerings, the appointed festivals***, the holy things, the sin offerings to atone for Israel, and for all the work of the house of our God.*

Isaiah 1:13-14 *Stop bringing useless offerings. Your incense is detestable to Me.* **New Moons and Sabbaths, and the calling of solemn assemblies** *— I cannot stand iniquity with a festival. I hate your New Moons and prescribed festivals. They have become a burden to Me; I am tired of putting up with them.*

141

Ezekiel 45:16-17 *All the people of the land must take part in this contribution for the prince in Israel. Then the burnt offerings, grain offerings, and drink offerings for **the festivals, New Moons, and Sabbaths** — for all the appointed times of the house of Israel — will be the prince's responsibility. He will provide the sin offerings, grain offerings, burnt offerings, and fellowship offerings to make atonement on behalf of the house of Israel.*

Hosea 2:10-11 *Now I will expose her shame in the sight of her lovers, and no one will rescue her from My hands. I will put an end to all her celebrations: her **feasts, New Moons, and Sabbaths** — all her festivals.*

Recall Colossians 2, not to let anyone judge us on questions of food and drink, or with regard to a festival or a new moon or a Sabbath because these are a shadow of the things to come, but the substance belongs to Christ.

We know that *"the kingdom of God is not eating and drinking, but righteousness, peace, and joy in the Holy Spirit"* (Rom. 14:17). So our focus is on what remains. This pattern of days refers to all of the holy days of the Jews, from yearly feasts to the weekly Sabbath, and comes from repeated descriptions of the Mosaic ritual as shown above. How does it make sense to claim the weekly Sabbath is not part of this summary? Only by blindly following a systematic theology wherein the Jewish weekly Sabbath has been re-skinned as the "Christian Sabbath" is this possible – but that does NOT make it biblical!

Scripture reinforces this idea, that days are not "holy" in the Christian faith, but a matter of personal conviction. Romans 14:5-6a *"One person considers one day to be above another day. Someone else considers every day to be the same. Each one must be fully convinced in his own mind. Whoever observes the day, observes it for the honor of the Lord."*

If you think Sunday is a holy day, observe it for the honor of the Lord. That does not provide a platform to condescend toward those who consider every day to be the same. As one who is in this latter category, I see the gathering of saints (usually on Sunday) as a holy thing; not the day. Same with the day of the Lord's resurrection – what took place that day is holy, the day is not.

Holy People, not holy places.

In John 4, Jesus went to Samaria to meet the woman at the well. The following conversation is foundational to the topic at hand.

John 4:19-24 *"Sir," the woman replied, "I see that You are a prophet. Our fathers worshiped on this mountain, yet you Jews say that the place to worship is in Jerusalem." Jesus told her, "Believe Me, woman, **an hour is coming when you will worship the Father neither on this mountain nor in Jerusalem.** You Samaritans worship what you do not know. We worship what we do know, because salvation is from the Jews. But an hour is coming, and is now here, when the true worshipers will worship the Father in spirit and truth. Yes, the Father wants such people to worship Him. God is spirit, and those who worship Him must worship in spirit and truth."*

A major point of all religions other than the one true one is that they have sacred places they must meet for worship. YHWH had met with the ancient Hebrews in the tabernacle. Their males went to Jerusalem three times a year to meet with God. Pagans built temples and altars at which they had to worship. In Acts 19 we see the pagan temple of Artemis (or Diana, depending on your translation) – the place was important.

In the passage from John 4, Jesus continues to introduce His kingdom by pointing out contrasts between it and what was being made obsolete. *"Believe Me, woman, an hour is coming when you will worship the Father neither on this mountain nor in Jerusalem."* This statement would have shocked both Jew and Samaritan, whose religions were based on sacred places. The kingdom of Christ is not of this world (John 18:36) and His people are to worship anywhere and anytime, as long we worship Him in spirit and truth. This is what YHWH desires – not ritual discipline to be at the temple at the right time.

During the ministry of Jesus and His apostles, we read of them engaging Jews in the Jewish synagogue (a system of worship developed outside of the canon of Scripture) but not worshiping with the Jews. When the saints met for worship, there is no record in Scripture of special places they were to meet. There are records of what they did and Who they worshiped.

We read in the Psalms how the people of Israel sang about meeting in the house of God. We read in the New Covenant passages how we are the house of God. Certainly, Christ's cryptic words *"destroy this temple, and in three days I will raise it up again,"* refer immediately to His bodily resurrection. But the Apostles of the New Testament also understood Christ's bodily *"temple"* in a metaphysical sense as a transcendent type of the corporate body of the elect who, as Christ's spiritual *"body"* or *"temple,"* were *"raised up together"* and *"made to sit together in heavenly places in Christ Jesus."* (Eph. 2:6) Thus James describes the salvation of Jews and Gentiles as the rebuilding of *"the tabernacle of*

David" (Acts 15:16); Peter refers to the regenerated church as *"living stones ... built up a spiritual house"* (1 Pet. 2:5); and Paul, as we have seen in Ephesians, depicts the present state of the church as a *"building fitly framed together"* which constitutes the *"holy temple of the Lord."* (Eph. 2:21)

The first ten verses of Hebrews 9 details how the tabernacle was a symbol for that present time, when ritual offerings which could not perfect the worshipers' conscience were made. Verse 10 sums it up: *"They are physical regulations and only deal with food, drink, and various washings imposed until the time of restoration."* Physical things relate to earth-bound religions. The time of restoration refers to the coming of the kingdom that was inaugurated by the death and resurrection of Christ Jesus. Verse 11 declares Jesus *the high priest of the good things that have come – the greater and more perfect tabernacle not made with hands (that is, not of this creation)*. The tabernacle in the wilderness was a sacred meeting place for the Hebrew people. Later they would sing about worshiping God in His house – the temple they had built. Another sacred place. Each child of God being a living stone, being built up into a spiritual house has no attachment to any geography. The places God's redeemed meet to worship Him is not important; having the people He has redeemed worship Him in spirit and truth is.

The spiritual is always greater than the temporal. Our citizenship is in heaven (Phil. 3:20) and those whose main focus is on temporal things are enemies of the cross of Christ (Phil. 3:18 & 19). The point is that whether we have large barns that satisfy our soul or put our treasures into grandiose buildings for saints to gather in, having our focus on earthly things is damaging to our souls. If we have been given much, we ought to give much; whether it's money, time, love, or fellowship. This is how we use temporal wealth – to aid those who are hurting, not to build grandiose buildings to impress people.

Philemon 3:13-15, 20-21 *Brothers, I do not consider myself to have taken hold of it. But one thing I do: Forgetting what is behind and reaching forward to what is ahead, I pursue as my goal the prize promised by God's heavenly call in Christ Jesus. Therefore, all who are mature should think this way. And if you think differently about anything, God will reveal this also to you. ... our citizenship is in heaven, from which we also eagerly wait for a Savior, the Lord Jesus Christ. He will transform the body of our humble condition into the likeness of His glorious body, by the power that enables Him to subject everything to Himself.*

The Christian faith is not food or drink, holy places or holy days. It is righteousness, peace, and joy in the Holy Spirit, which every child of God should recognize, enjoy, and praise God for His continued goodness towards us. Our predilection with calendars should not color over our focus on the One who saves sinners.

Bibliography

1644 London Baptist Confession

1646 London Baptist Confession

1689 London Baptist Confession

Anderson, James N., "A Tabular Comparison of the 1646 Westminster Confession of Faith, the 1658 Savoy Declaration of Faith, the 1677/1689 London Baptist Confession of Faith and the 1742 Philadelphia Confession of Faith"
 http://www.proginosko.com/docs/wcf_sdfo_lbcf.html

Ames, William, *A Marrow of Theology*, trans. John Dykstra Esuden, Grand Rapids: Baker Books, 1997

Britannica, Toleration Act,
https://www.britannica.com/event/Toleration-Act-Great-Britain-1689

Brogden, Stuart L., *Captive to the Word of God*, (Brogden's Books, La Vernia, Texas, 2017)

Brogden, Stuart L., *The First London Baptist Confession of Faith*, (Brogden's Books, La Vernia, Texas, 2020)

Brown, Louise Fargo, *The Political Activities of the Baptists and the Fifth Monarchy*, (Brogden's Books, La Vernia, Texas, 2021)

Bruce, Dustin, "The Intellectual Origins of the 1644 London Baptist Confession"
https://andrewfullercenter.org/media/blog/2013/03/the-intellectual-origins-of-the-1644-london-baptist-confession

Busher, Leonard, *Religion's Peace*, (Brogden's Books, La Vernia, Texas, 2017)

Calvin, John, *Calvin's Commentaries*. (Trans. John King. 22 vols. Edinburgh: Calvin Translation Society, 1844–1856. Repr., Grand Rapids, MI: Baker, 2005).

Bibliography

Christian History Institute, Article 7,
https://christianhistoryinstitute.org/incontext/article/polycarp-testimony

Clevenger, Steve, "1689 London Baptist Confession", (Covenant Reformed Baptist Church, Warrenton, VA, 2014)

Dyck, Cornelius J., "Waterlander Confession of Faith (1577)" https://www.anabaptistwiki.org/mediawiki/index.php?title=Waterlander_Confession_of_Faith_(1577)

Danker, Frederick W. and Bauer, Walter, *A Greek-English Lexicon of the New Testament and other Early Christian Literature*, (University Of Chicago Press, 2000)

Estep, William R., *The Anabaptist Story: An Introduction to Sixteenth-Century Anabaptism* (Grand Rapids, MI: William B. Eerdmans Publishing Co., 1963; reprint 1975, 1996)

Estep, William Roscoe, *Law And Gospel In The Anabaptist/Baptist Tradition*, (Grace Theological Journal 12.2 (1991) 189-214

Founders Ministries, Authors Page,
https://founders.org/author-name/sam-renihan/

Goadby, J. Jackson, *Bye-Paths in Baptist History*, (Elliot Stock, Paternaster ROW, E.C., 1871)

Hobson, Paul, *Practical Divinity: OR A HELP THROUGH the blessing of God to lead men more to look within themselves, and to unite experienced Christians in the bond and fellowship of the Spirit*, (Licensed and Published according to Order. And sold by R. HARFORD at the Bible in Queenes-head-alley in Pater-noster-row, 1642)

Hobson, Paul, "Spirit Distinctions", (1666)

Ivey, Michael N., *A Welsh Succession of Primitive Baptist Faith and Practice,* (Self published, Denton, TX 1994)

Kastler, Shane, "Comparing The Confessions: The History of the 1646 & 1689 London Baptist Confessions of Faith" (unpaginated article). https://shanekastler.typepad.com/pastor_shanes_blog/2014/07/comparing-the-confessions-the-history-of-the-1646-1689-london-baptist-confessions-of-faith.html

Kiffin, William, *Certain Observations upon Hosea the Second*, (1642)

Kiffin, William, *Remarkable Passages in the Life of William Kiffin*, (Editor: William Orme, Burton and Smith, London, 1823)

Long, Gary D., Preface to *The First London Baptist Confession of faith 1646 Edition*, (Sovereign Grace Ministries, Belton, Texas, 2004)

Lumpkin, William L., *Baptist Confessions of Faith*, (Judson Press, Valley Forge, PA, 1969)

Maxey, Zachary S., *Historical Forerunners of New Covenant Theology,* Providence Theological Seminary Journal, Issues 1, 2, 3, (Providence Theological Seminary, Colorado Springs, 2014 & 15)

McGlothlin, William Joseph, *Baptist Confessions of Faith*, (American Baptist Publication Society, Philadelphia, 1911)

Mickelson's Enhanced Strong's Dictionaries of the Greek and Hebrew Testaments, (LivingSon Press, 2015)

Patient, Thomas, *Doctrine of Baptism and the Distinction of the Covenants*, (Brogden's Books, La Vernia, TX, 2023)

PHILOSOPHICAL DICTIONARY – Subsistence, Substance, https://e-torredebabel.com/philosophical-dictionary-subsistence-substance/#:~:text=Subsistence%2C%20Substance.%20The%20former%20of%20these%20words%20is,by%20the%20majority%20from%20substo%2C%20to%20stand%20under

Reisinger, John, *Tablets of Stone & the History of Redemption*, (New Covenant Media, Frederick, MD, 2004)

Bibliography

Renihan, James, *A Tale of Two Associations*, (Fullerton, CA: Reformed Baptist Publications, 1997)

Renihan, James, "Confessing the Faith in 1644 and 1689" https://www.reformedreader.org/ctf.htm

Renihan, James, "No Substantial Theological Difference between the First and Second London Baptist Confessions", https://founders.org/articles/there-is-no-substantial-theological-difference-between-the-first-and-second-london-baptist-confessions/

Renihan, Samuel D., *From Shadow to Substance*, (PhD-Thesis - Research and graduation internal, Vrije Universiteit Amsterdam, 2017)

Ritor, Andrew, The Second Part of the Vanity & Childishnes of Infants Baptisme, (London, 1642)

Spilsbury, John, *A Treatise Concerning the Lawful Subject of Baptisme*, (Henry Hills in Fleet-Yardover against the Prison, London, 1652)

Waldron, Sam, *A Modern Exposition of the 1689 Baptist Confession of Faith*, (Evangelical Press, Webster, NY, 1989)

Vedder, Henry Cay, *A Short History of the Baptists*, (American Baptist Publication Society, Philadelphia, 1897)

Zens, Jon, "Is There a Covenant of Grace?" https://www.searchingtogether.org/articles/zens/covenant.htm

www.ingramcontent.com/pod-product-compliance
Lightning Source LLC
Chambersburg PA
CBHW071221090426
42736CB00014B/2927